Praise for

GET WEIRD

"Reassuring, moving, and practical, this book will help you embrace the magic you've always had."

—Seth Godin, author of *We Are All Weird*

"It's courageous and wildly creative, giving a voice to the misfit and make-believer in us all."

—Richard Rohr

"This book is a raw and soulful invitation to start imagining again and, along the way, rediscovering who we were actually created to be. What a gift!"

—Shauna and Aaron Niequist

"For close to a decade, I knew there was something weird and wonderful about CJ. Now he's got a quick road map that can help you discover the same path to ignoring the normal in favor of the fantastic."

—Jon Acuff, *New York Times* bestselling author of *Finish*

"This little book will brighten bookshelves and the world, because that's what weird things do. Whip-smart and full of heart, it is a needed wake-up call, an inspiring invitation to be unusual—because this world can't handle any more business as usual. CJ's mind operates in a wonderfully weird way and here he's gracious enough to let us in on the fun. It reads like a manifesto from a friend who be-lieves in you. That's because CJ really does care. I can't wait to see all the goodness that's unleashed in the world because of this weird and wonderful book."

—Brad Montague, writer, director,
and creator of *Kid President*

"This soulful and practical gem of a book will kick-start your imagination and embolden your heart. While the message in GET WEIRD will stay with you forever, you'll for sure give your copy away to a fellow weirdo. Better buy two now."

—Ian Morgan Cron, author of *The Road Back to You*

"A gifted poet who believes in the soul, CJ and his in-spiring book teaches us gradually about our own special gift of weirdness and how it can help minds change and communities heal. It's a huge gift to read his stories and walk with him as he discovers that being a square peg in a round hole keeps you from sinking. You will be blessed by this work."

—Becca Stevens, founder of
Thistle Farms and Episcopal priest

"For years CJ has been a champion of weirdos, misfits, and make-believers. If you find yourself with outrageous, beautiful, universe-altering ideas but have been afraid to try any of them for fear of what others might think, CJ is your weird whisperer. His words in GET WEIRD will nudge you (and sometimes give you one giant push) toward the wholeness you've been longing for as he guides you on an adventure full of rebels, rejects, boat rockers, and misbehavers to show you you're not alone. The good news: you're not normal. The better news: neither is the book."

—Mike Foster, founder of
People of the Second Chance

"In a world that is constantly telling us who we should be and what will make us happy, CJ invites us to be ourselves. It's a radical possibility, a much-needed authentic breath of fresh air."

—Jamie Tworkowski, *New York Times*
bestselling author and founder of
To Write Love on Her Arms

"I was not prepared for the gentle compassion with which CJ delivers his message of healing: that your weirdness is the thing that makes you sacred...and is what our world desperately needs now."

—David Hutchens, author of *Circle of the 9 Muses: A Storytelling Field Guide for Innovators and Meaning Makers*

"CJ's GET WEIRD meets you in the margins and celebrates you. Read with joy knowing you're beautifully made."

—Dave Gibbons, lead pastor at newsong.net
and founder of xealots.org

Get Weird

Discover the Surprising Secret

to Making a Difference

CJ CASCIOTTA

New York Nashville

FaithWords
Hachette Book Group
1290 Avenue of the Americas, New York, NY 10104
faithwords.com
twitter.com/faithwords

First Edition: September 2018

FaithWords is a division of Hachette Book Group, Inc. The FaithWords name and logo are trademarks of Hachette Book Group, Inc.

The publisher is not responsible for websites (or their content) that are not owned by the publisher.

The Hachette Speakers Bureau provides a wide range of authors for speaking events. To find out more, go to www.hachettespeakersbureau.com or call (866) 376-6591.

Illustrations on pages 33, 55, 83, 122, 170, and 202 by CJ Casciotta © 2018 by CJ Casciotta Productions Inc. All other illustrations © 2018 alxndr jones. avintagethought.com.

Unless otherwise noted scripture quotations are taken from the Holy Bible, New International Version®, NIV®. © 1973, 1978, 1984, 2011 by Biblica, Inc.® Used by permission of Zondervan. All rights reserved worldwide. www.Zondervan.com. The "NIV" and "New International Version" are trademarks registered in the United States Patent and Trademark Office by Biblica, Inc.™

Scripture quotations marked (esv) are taken from the ESV® Bible (the Holy Bible, English Standard Version®), copyright © 2001 by Crossway, a publishing ministry of Good News Publishers. Used by permission. All rights reserved.

Scripture quotations marked (msg) are taken from The Message. © 1993, 1994, 1995, 1996, 2000, 2001, 2002. Used by permission of NavPress Publishing Group.

Library of Congress Control Number: 2018944026

ISBN: 978-1-5460-3191-8 (trade paperback), 978-1-5460-3190-1 (ebook)

Printed in the United States of America

LSC-C

10 9 8 7 6 5 4 3 2 1

For Selah.
Go down the slides.

Contents

Introduction

I was sitting alone at a pub in New York City doodling some thoughts in a cup ring–stained notebook. The sidewalks outside were covered with the thinnest layer of snow, as if indecisive raindrops had changed their minds just before hitting the ground. I had come to New York to pitch a proposal that wouldn't pan out. Just a few months earlier, I'd been here to produce an event that would end up a complete disaster—one that would leave me riding back to my hotel on the subway repeating the line, "If I can make it here I'll make it anywhere" over and over in my head like some ironic, taunting joke.

Sitting there with my notebook under a blanket of white noise, a combination of clinking glasses and muffled conversations all orbiting my restless and weary brain, I wrote down a word that had never really presented itself to me with the significance it did in that moment.

Weird.

I was trying to make sense of my life and why every turn of events had seemed like entering a short hallway that led to a solid brick wall. I was a creative jack-of-all-trades, making a living on the rocky outskirts of a cubicle, helping companies with their communications and producing media for their campaigns, all the while trying to conjure up a few creative ventures of my own.

I knew what I was good at. I approached everything as a writer, a poet who believed there was such a thing as a soul, something divinely preinstalled, the source of people's greatest needs and longings.

A hippie prophet once told me my purpose in life was "to connect people to the person they are becoming." That was enough explanation for me, but a bit esoteric for a sales pitch, to say the least.

As I sat there hunched over a high-top table in my own dark little corner of Hell's Kitchen, I started thinking about the heroes of my childhood, guys like Jim Henson, Walt Disney, and Mister Rogers, the misfits and make-believers who had shaped my dream to one day make things half as good as they. I realized I was nowhere close, mostly because I hadn't even tried.

I glanced back down at that word *weird* again.

It started to come into razor-sharp focus.

I help people discover what makes them weird in a sea of sameness.

It was the heartbeat of how I had been helping companies. It was the character trait that linked all my heroes. It was the essence of all my fledgling creative projects. It was where I wanted to go in the future, a vision of helping as many people as possible, no matter their shape, size, or circumstance, understand what's unique about themselves and each other.

But wait a minute.

I peered down at the word again, this time staring at it until it blurred. *Weird.* I turned my head and noticed the crowd of drinkers around me, some on their first date, some undoubtedly on their last, some who had wandered in with the same restlessness I had, and others celebrating another sleepless night in a city that famously encourages every one of them.

I wasn't weird. I mowed my own lawn. I made dad jokes. I bought clothes with the precise purpose of fitting whatever wayward trend pop culture seemed to require at the moment. Who was I to assume this mantle of weirdness?

I flipped through my notebook, noticing all the doodles of monsters and imaginary creatures, scanning the random thoughts and poems I had always reassured myself were for "some other time."

Maybe it was time to get weird. Maybe it was time to reconnect with the sacred self my soul was busy scribbling in my notebooks. Maybe it was time to step off the safe and secure shores of Same and realize their promise was an empty one.

I had spent the past several years studying movements—how they start, grow, and create a sense of belonging among their followers, converting others along the way. I began sketching out in my notebook everything I had learned about how movements form, from Christianity to democracy to abolition, trying to distill it to its simplest form.

The through-line? You guessed it. All movements start off weird.

A stiff shot of clarity began to dance its way through my bloodstream. A distant passion drew closer and climbed into my nostrils like divine breath being blown into Adam. I was new again. Awake. Curious. Vital. If someone had taken notice of the disheveled, rigid man who walked into the bar, they would have wondered where he went and why a child was now sauntering out past a bewildered bouncer.

The subway sang a triumphant call as it pushed into the station. The doors flung open, offering a soundtrack to my personal renaissance. I didn't need to make it here. I had everything I needed.

I was weird. Everyone was. And I had to tell them.

Part 1

Why Are You So Weird?

Chapter 1

Who Told You You Were Naked?

It's strange to be here. The mystery
never leaves you alone.

—John O'Donohue

There's something different about you. Since the moment you arrived on planet Earth, you've been
carrying a unique combination of matter and spirit no
one else in human history could duplicate. And ever since
that moment, you've been told to ignore it.

I remember when my daughter was born. Shortly after taking her home from the hospital I was tasked with the duty of going to the local drugstore to pick up an extra package of diapers. I carried this out with both a deep sense of pride and bewilderment, as I imagined the young boys of World War II must've felt right before going into battle. Except I wasn't carrying a gun or wearing a uniform—just a debit card and a pair of skinny jeans along with an old Yankees cap I hadn't taken off since the first night in the hospital. Still, this was as close as I was going to get to those glory days when real men, like my grandfather, did brave things. The fantasy was holding up.

When I got to the drugstore, I carefully ran my finger across the packages that boasted a staggering number of options for an item with a very singular purpose until I found the fresh-out-of-the-oven newborn version. The only diapers available in newborn size had a famous mouse and duck printed on them. I couldn't believe it. I had but one option.

Apparently the mouse and the duck had met in a conference room with some diaper executives and negotiated a large sum of money for the ability to influence my daughter starting from the very first days of her life. Between large puffs on cigars followed by oversize-white-gloved handshakes, they hatched a plan to reach her unique, unblemished body with their form-fitting product.

She didn't stand a chance. None of us did.

From the time we are very small, when our souls are

still Play-Doh-like, we're persuaded by some outside force or another that it's better to fit in than to stand out. It's wiser, safer, and more prudent to color inside the lines, trace a perceived path, and conform to some pattern than it is to scribble our own shapes and arrive on our own shores.

For centuries prophets, priests, mystics, and poets have tried to name this temptress, this force that lures us into thinking our fulfillment is found in comparison and conformity. Some call it Sin. Some call it Resistance. Some call it the False Self. I'll give it a name as well: Same.

Same—meaning bland, homogenous, reproduced, discriminatory, and comparative.

We trust Same. We lean on it like a crutch. Same is safe.

But in the beginning, we were weird.

The word *weird* is often used as a way to reference those attributes that make us different, peculiar, or odd. The actual definition, however, holds far greater power.

Weird (adj.): involving or suggesting the supernatural; unearthly or uncanny.[i]

Weird isn't just this inconsequential word to be thrown around in jest or used to belittle someone we don't understand. *Weird* suggests the supernatural. *Weird* is unearthly. *Weird* is sacred.

In fact, try an experiment with me. The next time the word *weird* escapes your mouth, see if it's not a deeper invitation to suggest the supernatural. I've tried this over the past few months, and at least 50 percent of the time, I've noticed that what I was really conveying when I deemed something or someone *weird* was a veiled confession that I didn't understand what or whom I was talking about, that I was referencing something mysterious beyond my comprehension, something worth listening to, meditating on, and wrestling with.

In the ancient Hebrew language, there's a word for weirdness. It's called *qodesh* or "holiness," this idea of uniqueness, separateness, or, more specifically, set-apartness. It's a word the Jewish people associate with the concept of the Divine, the great Creator, the author of humanity, God. To them, to be holy is to align your soul (something they call *nephesh*) with the God who dwells within it.

In fact, in the Hebrew creation narrative, when the first humans disobey God, they suddenly become ashamed of their unique selves, scrambling to the bushes in an attempt to hide themselves from him.

Sound familiar?

Growing up in Sunday school, I must have encountered that story a hundred times in various primitive forms of media including puppet shows, cartoons, and flannel board presentations in which the first humans consistently had yoga bodies and white skin and stood conveniently angled so as to not reveal certain parts (I'd like to formally thank my Sunday School teacher, Miss Pigford, for introducing me to my first crush, Eve).

It wasn't until about twenty-five years later that this narrative took on a whole new dynamism for me. When I went back and read the original text in the book of Genesis, God's response to man's rebellion leaped off the page as if all those years in Sunday school had never transpired and I was hearing the story for the first time.

> God called to the Man: "Where are you?"
> He said, "I heard you in the garden and I was afraid because I was naked. And I hid."
> God said, "Who told you you were naked?"[ii]

Growing up in those stale, fluorescent-lit classrooms in the basement of some old Baptist church, I always assumed God's initial reaction to the first humans trying to be something they're not was anger. Years later, as a father, I can imagine the pain in his voice as the first thing he does is call out, "Where are you?" It's the picture of a father passionately searching for his children, an artist in active pursuit of what's missing. The very next reaction isn't admonishment or wrath, but rather profound disappointment and sorrow that someone had spread the lie to his creation that their custom-designed bodies and souls were somehow deficient, lacking, and, worst of all, needing to be covered.

It's a lie that still snakes around us to this day, the idea that our weirdness, our *qodesh*, needs to be covered up. From the earliest age we're trained to sit down, shut up, and comply with orders rather than stand up, stick out, and cause a disturbance. As young students we're taught getting the answers right is more important than asking the right questions. As adults we're culturally coached on what to buy, where to live, and how many kids to have.

Sadly, even many of our religious institutions are guilty of disseminating this message, spending far more time instructing people in how to act than awakening the unique *qodesh* in those who seek it.

There's something in our nature, both individually and collectively, that fights this proclivity we have to think outside the box, that attempts to relegate our imagination to books and films and computer games instead of applying it to real life, where it's a thousand times more useful.

It's our imagination, this God-given gift, reserved specifically for humans, that's responsible for our weirdness, the impetus, the nerve center of our *qodesh*. Whether we view ourselves as creative people or not, we're all born with an imagination that is actively at work in us when we're children. It's the place where rocket ships are created, giants are defeated, and the word *impossible* is never uttered, for if it were, we wouldn't know its definition. It's the part of our spirit, self, or soul where the question "What if?" resides impervious to the opinions and expectations of others.

When we started out as kids, it was as if our rational selves were unwelcome visitors we learned to put up with. We were more like imaginations weighed down by bodies that couldn't seem to catch up with our instinct to fly.

When I was six, my dad took me to see *Peter Pan* on Broadway. We lived on Long Island, right outside New York City, and I spent the entire train ride home processing out loud with him two very perplexing questions. The first one was, How could Peter Pan possibly be played by a girl, let alone a grown-up girl, when the Peter who flew around in my imagination was clearly a preadolescent male? The second and more easily answered question was, How were Peter and the other performers able to fly around inside the theater?

After chalking the first question up to "the art of acting," my dad, who always instinctively understood both my affinity for make-believe as well as my desire to be treated like a forty-five-year-old, explained that in order to fly the actors used a combination of wires, harnesses, and pulleys attached to the theater's ceiling.

Well, that was it. We just had to get one of those.

"Can we put one in our living room?" I asked with 100 percent seriousness.

When Dad said no, I spent the rest of the ride home trying to understand why this wasn't plausible. We had the perfect spot, above the casing that separated our dining room from our living room (which was often used as a stage for my performances). If a theater just miles away from our house had access to this kind of groundbreaking technology, the store where said technology was sold must be close by! I couldn't understand my dad's reluctance to agree.

"Is it a money thing? I could save up allowance. Or a safety issue? I'll save up another week for insurance!"

Years later, I'd be sitting in the audience watching another production of *Peter Pan*. My best friend was working for a Salvation Army center outside of Los Angeles and I came to support its after-school program, which was putting on a version of the play.

There was no flying in this one. Instead the parts were

played by little kids mostly from working-class families in the neighborhood. The production was pretty typical for a kids' show. There were cardboard props, homemade costumes, nervous monotone dialogue, and the occasional breaking of the fourth wall to wave to Mom.

But one facet of this production stood out to me. It was the character of Tinker Bell. Like the very flexible woman who played Peter Pan when I was six, this Tinker Bell did not fit the description of the character I had preserved for so long in my mind's eye. Tinker Bell, the traditionally dainty, blonde little fairy, was portrayed by a heavy-set Hispanic girl.

Don't you love that?

There was no conforming to patterns, no appeasing of Same. Just an honest representation of this beautiful young girl's one-of-a-kind identity—a girl who, in at least this instance, dodged the gavel of someone dictating who she can and can't be, fitting her into a box, and limiting her bandwidth. Sometimes I wish we saw that kind of directorial courage in our big, splashy Hollywood films.

I want to live in a world where Tinker Bell is portrayed as any shape, size, or color without us giving it a second thought, where the wild imaginations of our children aren't snuffed out by our weary struggle to maintain all things Same.

But before we can travel into that future together, we have to acknowledge that the past was quite the opposite for most of us. While we're wired for weird, we feel safer with Same. Same has been seducing our imaginations, lulling them to sleep for so long, that, like Lost Boys who've become pirates, we've woken up and discovered that we've forgotten how to fly. Before we can save the others, we must recognize that redemption, joy, creativity, belonging, the things we long for and dream about, don't reside at the end of a quest to conform, but deep inside the holy space that makes us particular, peculiar, and, dare I say, weird.

As a boy, with blood, sweat, and Crayola, I built worlds I longed to live in under bedsheets full of flashlight glow and marker stains I prayed were washable. Now I pray for those colors not to fade, for the light not to be extinguished. At some point, like most of us, I learned those worlds were best kept under cover.

The other day I was browsing in a bookstore when I noticed a girl who couldn't have been more than three or four years old sitting at a table in the children's section. She was busy coloring in a coloring book while her mother hovered over her. The girl's previously precise crayon-work suddenly and gloriously shifted as if a moment of wild inspiration had struck her. Moments ago she was caught in the details and minutiae of filling in tiny categories. Now she was furiously coloring outside the lines.

What happened next was both startling and yet all too predictable at once. Her mother leaned over the drawing and in a disapproving voice blurted, "Well, now you've ruined it."

She went on, her tone growing more chastising and shaming with every remark. "I'm not sure why you just did that. There's no saving it now. It's completely ruined."

The girl kept scribbling. The mother kept reproving. I kept trying to balance looking as if I weren't paying attention with the incredible urge to step in and do some serious "co-parenting."

The narrative that this small child will likely hold for a lifetime in her subconscious, the narrative that equates unconstrained wonder with contempt and detriment, is one that carries profound consequences, a story with no heroes, only villains.

I left the bookstore and began to judge her mother with the pious hubris of someone who had never done anything wrong to his own kid. A few moments into her imaginary sentencing hearing, shortly after I paused to remove a tree trunk from my eye socket, it occurred to me that perhaps she had grown up hearing similar admonishments. Perhaps she was simply transmitting a lie she herself was taught to believe was true. Perhaps she was once discouraged from coloring outside the lines. In fact, I'm sure of it. Because we all were.

At some tragic point, you shared what was inside your imagination out loud with someone and their response wasn't what you were expecting. They told you that it was weird. And they said it like it was a bad thing. They brushed it off, calling it idealistic, impractical, and foolish. And here's the crazy part: They were right. It was weird. It was foolish. And it was that way on purpose.

Dive deeper into those ancient scriptures I was first introduced to as a boy in Sunday school and you'll discover over and over again that God chooses the foolish things to confound those who think they know it all.[iii]

When we make believe as children do naturally, we're embracing our weirdness, or *qodesh*, tapping into what *could* be rather than endlessly striving for what should be. Perhaps this is why Christ says whoever refuses to see God's Kingdom like a child won't ever get in. When we abandon our weirdness, when we believe the lie that it's better to fit in than to stick out, we get further and further away from "on earth as it is in heaven." Creation stalls, evolution stops, and the status quo begins nestling comfortably for a long winter's nap.

But when we bravely decide to embrace our own weirdness, it lets others know they belong just as they are too. Our weirdness is contagious, viral, and generative.

Weird is what chose to spark the first fire, build the first bridge, fly the first plane, and capture the first film. Weird is what chose to stand up for the first injustices when no one else had the pluck to do so. Weird was what decided to turn classical instruments sideways, plug them into electrical sockets, and name it rock and roll.

Weird makes the world better. It's what moves it forward, pulling us along with it.

I have a younger friend who studied literature in college. We were at dinner one night and somehow Cervantes's *Don Quixote* came up. At the mention of the book, she launched into a speech praising what she thought to be the book's main theme: the absurdity of preserving traditions and ideals and how reality alone is the only thing worth trusting.

Maybe it's because I myself am a self-proclaimed hopeless idealist, but as I sat there listening to her go on about the book's message, I noticed my fists clenching up and my blood pressure rising, as if she were personally attacking a close friend of mine.

She was basically calling Don Quixote a loser.

I guess I'd never quite seen the story like that. Maybe she's right. But I also wonder if her literary professors simply disregarded Cervantes's nuance embedded between the lines of *Don Quixote*, this nonlinear, nonbinary idea that imagination and reality must somehow cohabit in order to produce a vibrant and sustainable culture. Sure, there's an idealism that robs us of contentment and acceptance, but there's also an imagination that ignites change, innovation, and movement, especially when it comes to how we view and treat each other as human beings.

Some might argue the risk isn't worth the reward, that Quixote's idealistic "madness" posed a threat to himself and others.

My friend Rob is a father of seven. He's committed his life to ending the trafficking and exploitation of children, traveling all around the world and putting himself in danger to combat one of the most horrific human rights abuses imaginable. He's one of my heroes. He once shared with me some of his favorite lines from *Don Quixote*: "When life itself seems lunatic, who knows where madness lies? Perhaps to be too practical is madness. To surrender dreams—this may be madness. Too much sanity may be madness—and maddest of all: to see life as it is, and not as it should be!"

These words keep Rob moving, keep him fighting, keep

him weird in a world that has settled for Same. Don Quixote isn't a complete loser. He's also a hero.

As the French-Lithuanian literary scientist Algirdas Julien Greimas once said in regards to Cervantes's protagonist: "Let's not be afraid to be Don Quixotes."[iv]

This is why we cry for Jimmy Stewart's character when we watch *It's a Wonderful Life*. It's why every other year, another Batman film comes out. It's why we hail Martin Luther King Jr. as a champion even when his outspokenness cost him his life. They're idealists, angry souls, dreamers with great expectations. And without them we'd be locked inside a prison of Same.

We need weirdness to keep the world moving, to help solve its problems, to change our minds and rattle our hearts. More specifically, we need your weirdness. Whether you're an artist, a teacher, a data processor, an engineer, or a mom, we need you to access and illuminate the *qodesh*, the Sacred Weird that rests deep within the corners of your soul—the ideas and passions you can't shake, the solutions you see that nobody else does, the one-of-a-kind history that only you carry, complete with all its crooked roads, cracks, and smudges.

Now, of course you may be reading this and feeling convinced that there's absolutely nothing weird about you. To you the very opposite seems true. Your life feels bland, mundane, almost painfully normal.

I once worked with a German woman who was absolutely convinced she wasn't creative because she was an administrator. In reality she was one of the more out-of-the-box thinkers I knew. The good news is, weirdness isn't something some people are born with and others aren't. Whether we like it or not, we are all weird, all misfits journeying together on the road to belonging. We all carry a unique set of stories and circumstances that not only shape us but shape others.

Your weirdness is your worth. It's the value you bring to this universe simply by breathing air with a set of lungs no one else has ever used before. You can't do anything to become weird, you must only acknowledge that you are weird, even when you don't feel like it—or when you would simply prefer to float gently in a giant sea of Same.

I'm guessing, however, that you picked up this book because somehow the word *weird* resonates with you. I'm guessing there's a world you imagine and long for that looks different from the one you currently belong to. I'm guessing at some point in your life you've been labeled an oddball, an outlaw, or an outsider. Perhaps you once possessed an active imagination, but it's become dormant in the wake of hard knocks and cold shoulders. Perhaps you've been told the strange way you look at the world isn't useful. Maybe you're unsure whether the things you long to create deep inside your soul have any value. Maybe you've been warned you ask too many questions. And because of that, maybe you're not convinced that your weirdness is there on purpose, that it's inside you for a reason, that's it's part of your *qodesh*, it's holy, it's sacred.

There's this scene at the end of *Robin Hood* (the Disney version where all the animals miraculously go ninety minutes without eating each other). King Richard, the kind and rightful ruler, returns, embraces Robin, who's married Maid Marian, and announces that he now has "an outlaw for an in-law." It's a beautiful picture of how I think God must feel about those who imagine a different world and are willing to break the rules to see that world appear, a world where justice, mercy, and kindness make their way to the poor and vulnerable through the weird work of outlaws, radicals, and rabble-rousers.

I wrote this book for the Robin Hoods. I wrote it for the Don Quixotes. I wrote it for the misfit idealists, those crazy enough to believe the future they imagine exists, even when it seems all hope is lost.

If you feel like an outcast, this book is for you. If you feel like an outsider, keep reading. If you feel like an outlaw, keep running.

Sanctuary is closer than you think.

Chapter 2

We Can Dance
If We Want To

I guess I've never been normal, not
what you call Establishment.

—Johnny Cash

Is it any wonder that the same God the Hebrews
described with the word *qodesh* goes on in those ancient scriptures to connect with humankind by
becoming a misfit? Like it or not, the movement of
Christianity began with one weirdo who attracted a

small tribe of fellow oddballs and eventually trans-
formed the world.

Personally, I love Jesus—not just his teachings, but because historically, he's one of the greatest examples of how
misfits start movements. Virtually everything about the
life and message of Christ is weird. He's born among farm
animals but claims he's the son of God, thinks he can save
Israel from being occupied without weapons, turns water into wine, speaks in riddles, and makes statements like
"Drink my blood and eat my flesh." His ideology was and
continues to be completely oppositional to whatever the
masses are currently pushing.

Consider for a moment the idea that the God who
spoke the universe into motion stepped onto planet Earth
to show humankind, if nothing else, that misfits matter.
The magic in Christ's movement is his restless, almost fa-
natical empowerment of those on the margins of society,
those just waiting in the crowds. These are the vehicles he
fuels with a mustard seed. As his father did with Adam,
these are the static combinations of matter and spirit he
breathes life into and tells, "Move."

Christ spoke to crowds as if he were speaking to his
close friends, and spoke with his close friends as if they
had the power to speak to the masses. Instead of picking
brilliant, capable, creative leaders of integrity, he went
after working-class drifters, test flunkers, soon-to-be trai-
tors, and crooked auditors. As with any movement, one
can propose he did this because he knew these were the
types of people his weird message would resonate with
the most, the ones looking to be identified, cared for,

and empowered to carry on his mission long after he left.

As I further explore later on, people with weird ideas have to work extra hard to hack into the "normalsphere," making their message applicable not just to misfits (who are usually early adopters), but everyone else as well. We see examples of Christ doing this kind of "normal hacking" peppered throughout the gospels: the way he turns a wedding crisis into a party, his gracious conversation with a skeptical rabbi named Nicodemus, and his actions during his life-or-death trial in front of Roman rulers who didn't even believe in the Hebrew God, let alone that Christ was his son. As much time as Christ spends with those who "get" him, he seems to have a special affinity for those who don't.

One of my favorite parables Christ tells is the one about the shepherd who goes after the lost sheep, found in the Gospel of Matthew. A shepherd who owns a hundred sheep suddenly realizes one of them has gone missing. In response he leaves the ninety-nine to search for the missing one until he finds it, carrying it back home in his arms. He is often known as the Good Shepherd, a caretaker who sees each individual member of his flock as equally important, worthy of a search-and-rescue operation even if it proves to be a liability, a risk others would scratch their heads at, wondering why it was worth the trouble.

I can't help but wonder if the sheep the shepherd went back for was the black sheep.

Earlier in that same gospel, people begin to label Jesus a drunk and a glutton because of the kinds of parties he'd frequent and the people who'd inevitably show up. I think one of the characteristics I like most about Christ is that he had an uncanny knack for being the life of the party without being the center of attention. His presence always seemed to be about something or someone else, concerned with a different angle or endgame from what everyone was expecting. His response to those overly religious types who couldn't seem to handle who, what, or where he spent time ministering was always, for lack of a better expression, so punk rock.

We played the pipe for you, and you did not dance; we sang a dirge, and you did not mourn.[v]

Jesus is basically saying, "Why don't you ever feel anything? Why don't you guys ever dance? You're such a slave to Same that you can't even recognize the beautiful reality before you: that truth is more like a wedding party than a DMV."

Have you ever watched a kid approach the dance floor at a wedding? At nearly every wedding reception I've been to (including my own) there seems to be at least one child who has absolutely no comprehension of the word *wallflower*. Without fail she rushes toward the dance floor, and as if no one in the history of the universe ever held an opinion, she dances. She moves her arms and legs with a flexibility that only someone whose bones have not yet been calcified by shame is capable of.

I think that kind of odd, unscripted, careless joy, the kind that bumps into people only to cause a conga line, is what Christ speaks of when he says, "We played the pipe for you, and you did not dance," a phrase Hebrew children would have easily identified with back in those days.

I want to learn to dance like that again. I've become a tin man, my joints locked into submission by my fear of moving them in a way others might judge. I want my life to suggest the supernatural, even if it means that some think I've become unhinged. I want to rush into the future my imagination sees the way a child rushes onto a dance floor, needing no invitation, intoxicated only by the liberty to move.

Perhaps this is why Flannery O'Connor once paraphrased the scripture in which Christ says, "You shall know the truth and the truth shall set you free" as "You shall know the truth and the truth shall make you odd."[vi]

There's this inextricable link between weirdness and freedom, an ability to recognize and rejoice in the fact that each of us is a little weird and somehow that shared weirdness sanctifies us.

Christ's revolutionary idea is that it's the misfits who inherit the earth, who can join the party simply by opting into it, an idea that opposes whatever protocol seems cemented in Same. It's a point of view many throughout history have adopted, sinners and saints, outlaws and outliers alike, one that ruthlessly and restlessly champions self-abandonment and love for the sake of a world we all imagine and secretly long for.

Why then, is it so hard for us to dance? What keeps us tin men, cowards, and scarecrows afraid of our true selves? Why is it so hard to stay weird?

Chances are, it's because your art teacher failed you.

But it probably wasn't her fault.

Chapter 3

Your Art Teacher Failed You

To educate the head without educating
the heart is to make moral monsters.
—*Report of the Faculty of Waterville
College on the Condition and Wants of the
Institution: With the Action of the Trustees on
the Same, at a Special Meeting of the Board,
Dec. 18, 1855*

When I was in kindergarten, my teacher sent us
home with a giant sheet of paper containing

illustrations of the parts that made up an apple. It was our job to go home, cut out the parts, color them in, and glue them all together so that they magnificently comprised one whole apple. She showed us what the finished product should look like: a red outline (the skin), with a white center (the fruit), and (this is important) a leaf for the stem.

I brought home my assignment and showed it to my mother, who played a massive role in shaping my creativity. I'm not sure where she got this idea, but she had decided no coloring books would ever be allowed in the house. Instead she would give me all the blank sheets of paper I wanted, a decision I couldn't be more grateful for today. Both my parents joked that I was single-handedly responsible for the deforestation of America, pointing to the massive amounts of paper displaying my creations that were constantly lining the floors and walls of our house.

My mother took one look at the illustrated sheet I had just brought home and noticed that "the leaf," as my teacher had named it, was not a leaf at all, but the core of the apple. I wasn't supposed to color it green. I was supposed to color it brown. I wasn't supposed to glue it on the outside, but in the center of the apple.

I'm not sure why my six-year-old brain struggled so much with this juxtaposition. Call it a natural predisposition to neurosis and anxiety (something that was cute then, and now just annoying), but I remember it rattled me. On the one hand, my mother, the authority figure I've come to know and love for six years, is calling something a core. On the other hand, this new authority figure, my kindergarten teacher, Ms. Klein, is clearly an expert in the field of apple composition. Otherwise they wouldn't be paying her the generous salary I was convinced teachers must receive.

What should I do? What if both of these authorities are wrong? Does the principal have an after-hours line I can contact? Can the PTA assemble to take a vote on this?

I think what unsettled me most was the idea of walking into class the next morning with an apple that was clearly different from everyone else's. I generally tended to trust my mother, but these were a new set of stakes. Not only would I be sticking out, I'd potentially be sticking out…and wrong. Even as a kindergartener I knew that Failure and Attention were ugly bedfellows.

After some discussion my mother convinced me to take my brown crayon to the leaf/core/potential self-esteem nightmare, set my Elmer's glue stick to optimum coverage, and stick it securely to the very center of the apple.

The next day I walked into school with my apple death sentence, along with a note from my mother attached to it, because if you're going to go down with the ship, why not do it while also holding a note from your mommy? The note explained to Ms. Klein her evident design flaw. Ms. Klein, a tired woman whose face often seemed to convey a "This is not what I signed up for" desperation, took a closer look at the so-called leaf and, with veiled embarrassment, announced to the entire class her mistake, declaring that it truly was a core.

I was relieved. But looking back at that day, I wonder

why I was so worried. What was it that made my little mind so averse to failure that I'd consider conforming to a rule that didn't even reflect reality?

I'm sure there are child psychologists who would say it was simply a classic case of fight or flight, but I wonder if it wasn't deeper than that. I wonder if I wasn't already starting to sense that the environment I found myself in (school, church, the playground) preferred a uniform way of thinking, concerned with everyone arriving at the same answers rather than daring to disrupt the pattern.

Educator Sir Ken Robinson puts it this way:

If you're not prepared to be wrong, you'll never come up with anything original. By the time they become adults, most kids have lost that capacity. They become frightened of being wrong. We run our companies this way, by the way. We stigmatize mistakes...and the result is that we are educating people out of their creative capacities.[vii]

This kind of culture, the culture we all belong to, can often feel like a giant game of Whac-a-Mole, that old arcade game where you win a prize for taking a mallet to any critter who pops up and sticks out. If you've ever been criticized for attempting to do something different, foreign, or potentially dangerous, you understand what I mean.

The unfortunate and wildly detrimental effect of this Whac-a-Mole culture we've created is that we've become fossilized by trepidation at the very thought of being wrong. School leaders run schools this way. Religious leaders run institutions this way. Politicians run governments this way. Same is safe and safe is primal. We've learned it's better not to rock the boat, even if doing so would help us build a better boat.

But building a better boat sounds an awful lot like arriving at the truth. And as we've already concluded, if we are going to be set free by truth, we're going to have to get weird.

How, then, did we become a people petrified by fear?

Once I discovered as a young adult that my entire education up until college had been centered around retaining the bare minimum amount of information to pass a state-required test each year, I felt cheated. No wonder the lights had long left my teachers' eyes by the time I sat down in their rigid chairs. No wonder we spent so little time on *why* the Civil War started and instead were simply quizzed on when.

We've been taught to mimic from a very early age, judged by what we were able to remember and reproduce, not what we were able to uniquely create.

But creativity is what moves the world forward. Uniqueness, weirdness, differentiation is what drives innovation and change.

I often wonder if this was why even my earliest memories of art class feel less like an exploration of what artists do or the value they bring to society and more like a commercial for Crayola. In fact, I don't think I can remember a single lesson in art class when a teacher explained that the primary function of art is to challenge the status quo, instigate discussion, change people's minds, and make them feel!

That's worth grieving.

The world is currently stockpiling a landfill of undiscovered artists because they were never taught to discover the creativity that lives within them.

"All children are artists. The problem is how to remain an artist once he grows up."[viii] It's as if the warning of Pablo Picasso has fallen on deaf ears.

I wish one art teacher, just one art teacher, had explained to me and my classmates the unadulterated truth that we are all intrinsically creative. It doesn't matter whether our imaginations are naturally bent toward engineering or architecture, function or form, the human body or the human spirit. It has no bearing whatsoever on the fact that we have an imagination in the first place, something that's there to solve problems, change paradigms, make believers out of skeptics, and so on.

Sure, art class came naturally to a guy like me, but what about Thomas, who wanted to be a physical therapist, Jill, who wanted to be a veterinarian, Caleb, who loved taking appliances apart and putting them back together, or Kate, who couldn't wait to be a mom one day?

To be clear, I think art teachers are remarkable. They're the underdogs of the educational system, marathon runners, unrelenting champions of beauty, culture, and creativity. There are plenty of art teachers making a massive difference in their students' lives, doing the very best they can in an environment that does little to support them.

What I'm getting at is a larger, foundational flaw in the way our culture values art in general, especially when it comes to what we teach our kids. If your art teacher failed you, it likely wasn't her fault. It was the system that relegated her discipline to a hobby, something cute the kids could bring home to show their parents and stick on the refrigerator.

In reality, it's so much more.

Many don't want to look at it, but there's a critical and urgent crisis on our hands. Studies show that by the year 2025, careers that once seemed like safe bets, such as office work, administration, and manufacturing jobs, will become increasingly difficult to find. On the other hand, skills like collaboration, caregiving, and social intelligence will grow in demand.[ix] The *Washington Post*, for example, recently reported that after conducting an extensive study, Google, one of the largest technology companies in the world, was shocked to find that attributes such as empathy, creativity, and emotional acumen were among the top qualities of its most successful employees.[x] These are the skills the next generation will need to develop in order to thrive in the modern workplace. However, 80 percent of US school districts have had their arts and humanities funds cut since 2008.[xi]

It saddens me to the level of righteous rage that we've divided up the vast and expansive field of learning into two wildly insufficient categories, the sciences and the arts, as if one can possibly exist without the other. Instead of looking for through-lines and intersections, we've siphoned off an entire collection of disciplines and labeled them "the humanities"—as if studying the natural order of things had nothing to do with studying the mystery of what it means to be human.

Science needs a question; otherwise it becomes a stagnant pool, void of any innovation or progress. A question needs freedom, release from the tethers of what is known. It needs a questioner, a doubt holder. A questioner needs permission to enter into that space where the rules are allowed to be played with, turned upside down, and at times even broken. Art is the only landscape adequate for this journey, because it knows and speaks the language of mystery.

Art needs an anchor, otherwise it becomes a vapor, evaporating away from tangibility. An anchor needs a foundation so that when art leaps into the unknown, it doesn't slip into obscurity. Science is the only soil befitting of this foundation, because it plants and grows the palette of the imagination.

As the future will prove, we aren't binary beings who ought to be studied in silos. We're mixtures, compounds, and cocktails. We're weird.

> *Natural things*
> *and spiritual,—who separates those two*
> *In art, in morals, or the social drift*
> *Tears up the bond of nature and brings death,*
> *Paints futile pictures, writes unreal verse,*
> *Leads vulgar days, deals ignorantly with men,*
> *Is wrong, in short, at all points. We divide*
> *This apple of life, and cut it through the pips,—*

....

> *Without the spiritual, observe,*
> *The natural's impossible;—no form,*
> *No motion! Without sensuous, spiritual*
> *Is inappreciable;—no beauty or power!*
> *And in this twofold sphere the twofold man*
> *(And still the artist is intensely a man)*
> *Holds firmly by the natural, to reach*
> *The spiritual beyond it.*

—from *Aurora Leigh* by Elizabeth Barrett Browning

In high school I couldn't stand chemistry class and avoided physics altogether. Lately I've been researching quantum physics for the fun of it. I realize now that I was simply a *why* person trapped in a *what* environment.

Whenever we remove the *why* from the *what*, we subtly threaten our innate ability to stick out and question whether something is a leaf or a core.

We are all artists. Each and every one of us. Our professions, our institutions, and our communities are full of counterfeit leaves. Art is the ability to see the core.

Ancient philosophers like Plato believed in the transcendentals, three main characteristics that transcend our individual lives and unite us all as human beings: beauty (or the arts), truth (or science), and goodness (or morality). Again, these were never meant to be silos, which has become the temptation if not the default. On the contrary, culture moves forward only when we triangulate these elements, realizing that goodness happens only when beauty and truth combine, that the path to truth is observing both beauty and goodness, and that when truth and goodness embrace, we stand in awe of their beauty.

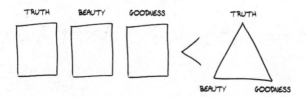

Is this not the reason we're so divided as a society in the United States? We've been implicitly told from the earliest age that questioning, dialoguing, risk taking, and feeling anything at all pales in comparison to following standards, punching in numbers, and checking the right boxes. We can't expect to erase generations' worth of this kind of neglect overnight. When people never learn how to feel—how to put their emotions, intuition, and inward thoughts into a context where they can properly express them—we are headed for a dangerous, dangerous future. We resort to weapons and drugs. We objectify our neighbors instead of acknowledging their souls. We hide our point of view behind a screen because we're not prepared to express it in 3-D.

When we don't know what to make of our weirdness, we can't appreciate it in others. Not only do we journey through existence feeling naked, exposed, and void of any sacredness or *qodesh*, we're completely unable to identify it in those orbiting around us.

In short, we feel afraid.

Chapter 4

When the Weird Went Away

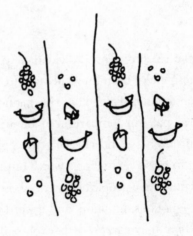

Never grow up....Always down.
—Roald Dahl

Thomas Merton, the weirdo beatnik monk who rose to unlikely fame during the 1940s, had this to say about the relationship between our weirdness (something he referred to as "sincerity" or "candor") and our fear:

Fear is perhaps the greatest enemy of candor. How many men fear to follow their conscience because they would rather form to the opinion of other men than to the truth they know in their hearts! How can I be sincere if I am constantly changing my mind to conform with the shadow of what I think others expect of me? Others have no right to demand that I be anything else than what I ought to be in the sight of God. No greater thing could possibly be asked of a man than this! This one just expectation, which I am bound to fulfill, is precisely the one they usually do not expect me to fulfill. They want me to be what I am in their sight: that is, an extension of themselves. They do not realize that if I am fully myself, my life will become the completion and the fulfillment of their own, but that if I merely live as their shadow, I will serve only to remind them of their own unfulfillment. If I allow myself to degenerate into the being I am imagined to be by other men, God will have to say to me, "I know you not!"[xii]

Oh, to be captives of our own imaginations and not the will of others. To be fully ourselves and not a shadow of someone else. Perhaps this is why Peter Pan desperately wanted his own shadow to stick. He knew that if it left him, he'd eventually be tempted to do what all grown-ups have learned to do: find someone else's shadow to step into.

As Saint Paul once warned the Romans living in the

first century, when we convince ourselves out of fear that our worth can be found only by conforming to patterns, we miss out on the gift of a greater awakening, a deeper understanding of our humanity, a transforming of our minds and souls.[xiii]

Theologian and contemplative Eugene H. Peterson paraphrases Saint Paul's warning this way: "Don't become so well-adjusted to your culture that you fit into it without even thinking. Instead, fix your attention on God. You'll be changed from the inside out."[xiv]

It seems that those truly close to God, those who have spent enough time steeped in their own weirdness quietly listening for the truth amid a sea of nonsense noise and television static, understand that if there is a God, he's a God of the square peg.

At some point, however, we lose our edge, beaten over time to conform to a round hole we were never destined for. Where were you when you got the weird kicked out of you?

I was in the fourth grade. Our class had just performed a skit as part of an assembly in front of the whole school. It was one of those multipurpose cafeteri-gym-atorium rooms every elementary school has, but being that our school was on Long Island, as far as I was concerned it was off Broadway.

As one of the actors, I'd looked over the script the night before, and, like some Jewish comedy writer from the 1950s, decided it was hack material and needed a rewrite. The following afternoon, during the performance, without any warning, I inserted some of my own material in a decision that seemed to go smoothly in the moment (as I remember, I got some laughs) but that I would come to regret shortly after.

If you were a kid in New York during the early nineties, you know that public schools were experimenting with something called "peer mediation," which is exactly what it sounds like. It was the idea that kids should be taught to solve their problems collaboratively—not just the specific kids in conflict with each other, mind you, but the entire class! This was a fine and noble idea, one I'm sure was carefully discussed around large Formica tables by people in padded chairs who examined every possible objection, with the exception of one crucial detail: we were fourth graders! It's as if no one in the conference room of whatever committee voted this method into practice had ever read *Lord of the Flies* to the end.

After the audience of students left, my teacher, Mr. D'Angelo, gathered our entire class around one of the tables in the now otherwise empty cafeteri-gym-atorium and proceeded to facilitate a discussion about the negative consequences of my action, how it caught the other performer off guard and made everyone uncomfortable.

Funny, Mr. D, I thought. *Was it anything like the way I'm feeling right now with you singling me out in front of everyone? Because I think we all get the picture.*

As a reminder, I'm in the fourth grade here—nine or ten years old. And it's not as if the whole class had been in the skit. It was just me and a girl. We were the only performers.

It's not Mr. D'Angelo's fault entirely. He was part of

a system that was urging him to do this kind of thing. Mr. D'Angelo was a soft-spoken, gentle man. His words of admonishment weren't angry or intentionally shaming. They were meant to be constructive and helpful, and he had only the common good in mind. The only problem was, this wasn't a one-on-one coaching moment, it was a team huddle.

As we walked back to the classroom in the best version of a single-file line twenty-five nine-year-olds could muster, I could sense the thick air of disdain from my peers, the conch shell smashed to smithereens. While we were walking toward the cubbies to gather our backpacks and other belongings, one classmate brushed past me and muttered, "Way to go, CJ." Another classmate joined in, "Yeah, nice job, Casciotta." Soon a whole chorus of kids were echoing this sentiment of disapproval for my inappropriate ad-lib.

That was it. I couldn't hold it in any longer. I broke down and cried.

As early as the fourth grade I had learned my lesson: stick out and you'll regret it.

I'm not saying what I did shouldn't have gone uncorrected. I'm not saying it wasn't insensitive to the other person in the skit. It probably wasn't the most effective strategy for taking the play all the way to Forty-Second Street (I'm not sure, I never read the review from the *New York Times* critic I'd invited to come). But here I was, a sincere kid full of unbridled creativity, weird ideas, and pluck—and instead of all that being harnessed and steered, it was stomped on.

Our weirdness is our sincerity. It's the pure, unadulterated "what if" we bring to the world. I think it's why Linus determines that the Great Pumpkin will undoubtedly visit the pumpkin patch that is "the most sincere." What a fitting environment for the hero of a child's weird imagination, standing alone while others make fun and opt for a normal night of trick-or-treating. I've always loved everything made by Charles Schulz, the creator of Linus and the rest of the Peanuts gang. It's all soaked in sincerity. From Charlie Brown's optimistic belief that Lucy won't pull away the football to his hopeful determination to fly his kite without crashing it into some tree, Schultz always stood up for the everyman, seeing him as brave, calling out the Don Quixote that lives inside every kid and every kid at heart. His work reminds us that to be sincere is to be honest, pure, optimistic, and hopeful. And, unfortunately, those qualities are often branded as foolish, feeble, and moronic.

Most of us get the weird kicked out of us before we ever really get a chance to cultivate it for good. No wonder we often associate the word *weird* with negative feelings and ideas we'd rather push to the margins.

Remember that scene in *Willy Wonka & The Chocolate Factory*? (The movie is such a campy, psychedelic interpretation of Roald Dahl's classic story, so *seventies* in every way, but I love it. It's inextricably woven into the fabric of my childhood memories.) Played perfectly by Gene Wilder, Wonka, while explaining a new candy invention, remarks, "The snozzberries taste like snozzberries!" One of the kids, a bratty, entitled little girl, interrupts and indignantly asks, "Who's ever heard of a snozzberry?"

If you've ever made a decision to step outside of a box, color outside the lines, or do something weird, you've come across that question.

You may have received a smug "I don't get it" or the earnest but deadly classic "We've never done it that way."

If this has happened to you, congratulations. You've encountered what I like to call "the snozzberry effect." You've inserted your token into the Whac-a-Mole arcade game only to discover that you, unfortunately, are the mole.

I once heard someone say that people who do really interesting work often walk with a limp. There's a loneliness, a scarcity, a tension weirdos feel as they sail out over a dark and stormy sea of Same.

* * *

I met Charlie about three years ago. Charlie is a Tennessee native, in his thirties, and quite possibly the most fascinating person I've ever met. My wife hired him to build a bench for our dining room after responding to an ad he put out online. When he delivered the bench a few weeks later he told us he had built it by hand without any power tools, just the collection of manual tools he'd inherited after his grandfather passed away. While Charlie's overall posture was humble and meek, his eyes beamed with pride as he mentioned that the wood came from the hardwood floors of an old distillery his uncle once owned.

This was much more than we had been expecting when we agreed to hire someone to make us a bench. We stood there in disbelief at the one-of-a-kind story and craftsmanship of a piece we'd paid only a couple hundred bucks for. When we asked Charlie why such a unique creation had cost us so little, he replied that this wasn't his full-time gig, that he was just getting this side business off the ground, and the best payback we could possibly give him was to tell others.

We did, but not without commissioning him for more projects ourselves.

As Charlie would continue to drop by, delivering new batches of reclaimed stories one after another, we started forming a friendship. I learned that his day job was as a police officer in one of the more dangerous sections of Nashville but that he was looking for a way out. I learned that he used to be a military sniper and had only recently returned home from duty in the past few years. I learned that he owned a horse farm with about fifty acres of farmland he looked after himself.

I had to pry these mind-boggling facts out of Charlie. Believe me when I say he is the very definition of the word *understated*. He's humble and self-effacing to an almost incomparable degree. It's no secret to anyone I know that one time I valiantly broke my pinkie toe after crashing it into the baseboard outside our bedroom accidentally. I can't imagine I'd keep any one of Charlie's accomplishments a secret, even from strangers. I'd pester the cashier, the barista, and even the meter maid with tales of my horse farm and days as a government-paid sniper.

Looking at Charlie, though, he doesn't come off as the Rambo, rough-and-tumble warrior type. He's tall, lanky, baby faced, friendly, and quiet.

Once I'd dug enough information out of Charlie during his many drop-off visits to be thoroughly and utterly amazed that one human being could have accomplished so much, I asked him if he wanted to grab a couple of beers one night so I could learn more about this Mister Rogers–meets–Clint Eastwood crazy man.

It was the last week of December. The air was crisp but not yet raw, as if to exhale the last few breaths of Christmas before surrendering to the New Year's cold birth. Over rounds of stout Charlie unloaded what could have been seven different movie scripts, each a blockbuster in its own right.

He told me about the time he was training as a sniper and pulled "a Robin Hood," literally splitting a dowel that held up his mark over seven hundred yards away. He told me about the time he went over his boss's head on the police force, devising an "extracurricular" plan to take down Nashville's sex traffickers, partnering with other officers to perform undercover sting operations in motels. He came up with the idea of hiding an undetectable camera inside the alarm clock that sat on every hotel room nightstand, a game changer that led to a stream of successful arrests.

If you can believe it, he recounted all of this without a drop of ego or awareness that anything he had done was remotely extraordinary.

I mean, it's one thing to be humble, it's another to be

dispirited. Charlie seemed more the latter. A few more questions later, I'd come to find out why.

Charlie had gotten the weird kicked out of him.

While his grandfather fostered a love for woodworking in him as a boy, Charlie's dad belittled his creative projects, at times even commanding him to remove his artwork from the walls. At the peak of his performance as a sniper, Charlie was forced to leave the military after injuring his ankle playing soccer. Once back home, he found it difficult to land even an entry-level job. It didn't matter that while in the army, Charlie had learned leadership, management skills, integrity, and teamwork. It didn't matter that he was arguably the very best marksman in the country. It turns out those qualities don't mean much to Same-obsessed potential employers at big-box chains or warehouse suppliers. After months of searching, Charlie did finally manage to land an opportunity to train for the police force.

Once on the force, he struggled his way through politics as he fought to reconcile the difference he knew he could make with the "don't rock the boat" culture pressed upon him.

To top that, his young wife proceeded to have an affair before finally deciding to leave Charlie, who had been nothing but faithful throughout their marriage.

In the course of a few minutes, as the lights dimmed over our booth in that noisy pub, this woodworking, gun-slinging, crime-fighting, horse-farming, all-American hero who'd had it all in my mind's eye had become a living, breathing country-and-western song.

I went to the bathroom to collect my thoughts and try to make sense of everything Charlie had just told me.

When I came back he had paid for my beer. Classic Charlie.

It's sobering to think that even someone like Charlie could roam this life among so many who couldn't see the value of his weirdness. Here I am, average, scrawny, unathletic, a real measure-once, cut-twice kind of guy, writing a book about weirdness. I get why people might overlook my value. I get what they might not see in me. But Charlie? Winnie-the-Liam-Neeson-with-a-Particular-Set-of-Skills-Pooh Charlie? It's as if it's easier to blind ourselves to the value of what we don't understand than to understand why we've gone blind.

If Charlie can push past the undeserved rejection he's encountered, if he can feel like a misfit in a world that should deem him a hero and still find the Sacred Weird coursing through his veins enough to pick up a hammer, put on a uniform, or plow a field, then the rest of us certainly can follow his example.

We all feel the bricks on our chest stacking up one by one with each journey from summer to winter. We're all learning what it's like to quietly acknowledge the truth that something's missing, something's off, something's heavy. We all know something got beaten...but that something is still fighting for its life.

Weird doesn't quit on us. We quit on it. Better put, we give others the power to extinguish its light.

Do you remember how Wonka replies to the girl who can't possibly imagine the existence of a snozzberry? He doesn't ridicule or belittle her. He doesn't stoop to her level or play the victim.

Wonka grabs her by the cheeks, looks her dead in the eye, and begins quoting from "Ode," a poem by the English poet Arthur O'Shaughnessy: "We are the music makers, And we are the dreamers of dreams."

Here's the first verse of that poem in its entirety:

We are the music makers,
And we are the dreamers of dreams,
Wandering by lone sea-breakers,
And sitting by desolate streams;—
World-losers and world-forsakers,
On whom the pale moon gleams:
Yet we are the movers and shakers
Of the world for ever, it seems.

"Ode" actually contains the first occurrence of the phrase *movers and shakers* documented in literature. What the prophet Wonka and the poet O'Shaughnessy both seem to suggest is that those few bold enough to birth their weird ideas and nurture them into the universe, those who refuse to step into someone else's shadow, will often be met with skepticism, looked at as losers, and left alone. You can bet your money on that and come out rich every time.

Ultimately, however, these are the very weirdos who will move the world forward, shake it by the lapels, grab it by the cheeks, and play for it a brand-new song.

Chapter 5

The Parable of the Ugly Cactus

The true work of art is but a shadow of
the divine perfection.
—Michelangelo

It could be better."

Those were the words Jody grew up hearing from her father.

From as early as she could remember, Jody was determined to become an artist. What began on floors full of finger paints and construction paper eventually evolved to time spent with easels, oils, brushes, and canvas. Throughout high school and college, Jody poured every ounce of herself into her artwork, practicing, experimenting, and absorbing all the information, instruction, and critique she possibly could.

After completing a piece, she'd bring it home to her father, a successful doctor where they lived in New Mexico. His response never wavered.

"It could be better."

I met Jody because she married one of my best friends, John. We all had watched him go from girl to girl, some with "crazy eyes," others with jealousy complexes. When John finally met Jody, we all knew she was the one, a perfect yin to John's yang. She was relaxed and fun but strong and determined, equally comfortable standing her ground and letting others shine.

Jody and John recently traveled to Nashville to visit us on vacation. It was great to see them. They're the kind of friends you don't have to try with, the kind you don't have to impress or perform for, those rare soul siblings you can let down your guard in front of.

Since her days studying and practicing fine art, Jody has spent most of her adulthood as an accomplished fashion designer, creating patterns and styles for some of the world's most popular brands. It's a demanding, stressful environment, but one her personality navigates with finesse. One evening over dinner and drinks while John and she were in town, Jody shared with me that she was wanting something different. She had spent the entirety of her twenties trying to stuff down the Sacred Weird within her, but despite her best efforts, it kept rising back to the surface like a balloon.

She liked her job, but she was growing tired of spending the majority of her time creating patterns. She wanted to get weird. She wanted to reintroduce herself to the curious child who had once painted and sketched without hesitation or guilt. She wanted to fall asleep at night with color-stained hands only to wake up with an insatiable passion to put those hands to greater, more meaningful work than the day prior.

She started to recount the passion for art that had introduced itself to her as a child. When she recalled her father's predictable words, her eyes locked on some identified specter beyond my peripheral, she quickly qualified those words by adding how wonderful a motivator they had been, how they had pressed her to keep striving, developing, and inching toward greatness.

I believed her. How could I not? How many of us have accomplished remarkable feats because we saw some carrot dangling at the end of a stick? How many of us have almost involuntarily opted in to a grand and maddening chase to win affection and validation from someone we love and wish to please? Books are written this way. Businesses are traded and sold for this reason. I'm convinced even presidencies are won with this in mind. Shame, it turns out, is a mighty motivator. But shame has a short shelf life, one that often ends in its victim wanting more than they bargained for. There's a fine line between "It could be better" and "Better play it safe."

It'd been years since Jody held a brush to a canvas.

Long commutes and short deadlines made doing so seem impractical, even luxurious. But lately, the urge had just been too strong.

Over the dim light of a small table candle, Jody leaned in as if to tell a ghost story around a campfire and admitted, somewhat sheepishly, that she had recently begun to paint again.

"Before we left town, I bought some brushes and some watercolors and I started to paint a cactus."

"That's great!" I said. "I'm so proud of you. I'd love to see it when it's done."

"Well," she replied quickly as if trying to delete her last sentence. "It's a pretty ugly cactus."

I now knew who the apparition just out of my sight was. Jody was two thousand miles away from that dry desert she'd grown up in with her family, the rigid rules and expectations that had marked the beginnings of her soul's journey, but as far as she was concerned, her father might as well have been sitting in the room with us.

Regardless of his intention, Jody's father had unfortunately reinforced the belief that the purpose of art, our identity translated to and through the senses, the expression of the Sacred Weird within us, is to arrive at some apex of validation and approval. From Jody's perspective, art was a fixed goal that one could plot toward if one worked hard enough while staying in a straight line.

That, of course, isn't true. In reality, the primary purpose of any kind of art is to awaken what needs to be expressed in us and those around us.

There is a far greater need for people to see an "ugly"

cactus, one that's weird and unrefined, than there is for them to observe a "perfect" one (as if such a thing ever existed in the first place). Consider which would have a greater impact on someone: simply observing a near-photographic reproduction of a plant or knowing that someone just like them, someone with the same fears and insecurities, who juggled the same busy schedule and priorities, had the guts to pick up a brush? After years of separation and avoidance, is it not more compelling to watch Jody try, to see her live with the fleet of negative voices circling the fences of her soul, and create anyway?

That's the kind of creativity that moves us, that illuminates our own Sacred Weird, covered by cobwebs, and whispers, "I see you."

We desperately need to see your crooked branches and your prickly edges accompanied by your blots, your blemishes, and your surprising twists to be reminded of who we really are and why it matters. We need you to remind us that life is capable of springing up from the driest desert, that we might dare to look for the living among the dead.

This must be why the God of those old Sunday School scriptures takes on the character of a parent, one who doesn't respond with, "It can be better," but with something far more effective and sustainable: "I see you."

Please don't confuse the two.

I'm not saying every one of us should automatically receive a trophy. I'm not saying we should never seek to improve our skills and abilities. I'm saying there is a deeper, more underlining motivator that doesn't just settle for incremental improvement but sparks transformative resurrection.

The perfect parental response (one we can attempt to echo as mothers, fathers, teachers, and coaches) is this:

"I see you."
"Come forth."
"Keep going."

"The grave, the cave, the hiding, and the shame—they're not for you, not where you belong. You belong to us in the sunlight where you can grow and sow and nourish yourself to life. We are not afraid of your stumbling steps. We're afraid we'll never know you if you choose not to take them."

Sitting at that restaurant table, I shared all this with Jody, trying to temper the passion from leaking all over the place, spilling the water glasses and flinging the silverware on the floor. John sat by her side in quiet affirmation. For a moment, we were all silent. A few seconds later, strange moisture started leaking from all three pairs of our eyes.

I couldn't believe one stupid little ugly cactus made us do that.

Chapter 6

The Myth of the Caterpillar

Human salvation lies in the hands of
the creatively maladjusted.
—Martin Luther King Jr.

I sat there staring at the television screen, my mouth agape and nearly touching the carpet. My three-and-a-half-year-old daughter was sitting next to me, blissfully watching the clay puppets glide across a coarsely painted set.

I couldn't believe it. All my life I'd been peddled a lie.

Every parent knows that part of the magic of having kids is reliving your favorite childhood experiences with them. So when December came I couldn't wait to fire up *Rudolph the Red-Nosed Reindeer* and show her what good old-fashioned 1960s commercialism was all about.

I hadn't seen the movie in years but remembered that it had seemed to ceremoniously usher in the Christmas season each time it came on TV.

As I watched it with my daughter now, my new instinct was to shut it off and hope she never wanted to see it again.

I know what you're thinking: "What could possibly be wrong with sweet, lovable Rudolph?" Well, allow me to air my grievances.

First of all, Santa Claus is a jerk. I mean a real blowhard. When he comes to visit Donner and his wife, who's just given birth to Rudolph, he's appalled at the baby's glowing red nose and warns Donner that it had better stop if he's ever going to be on Santa's sleigh team—for what reason we're never told. This sends Donner into an existential panic, the same one often seen in fathers who coach their sons in soccer or Little League—as if Rudolph's perceived failure is somehow an extension of his own.

In response, Donner covers Rudolph's nose in black clay to hide its light. When his wife (whose name we're never actually given) objects, she is quickly silenced by Donner, a reaction that assures the audience of who wears the antlers in the family.

Santa is a griping, grumpy, ungrateful old man who

doesn't have much kindness to show toward Mrs. Claus, whose only reasons for existence seem to be feeding him and softening the blow after he belittles his workforce for a less-than-perfect performance of "We Are Santa's Elves."

This is supposed to be the arbiter of moral aptitude? This is the guy we've given permission to decide whether our children have been naughty or nice?

My biggest issue isn't just with Santa, though; it's with the entire arc of the story.

But wait a minute! I thought the story of Rudolph was about a misfit who realizes the very thing that makes him weird is the thing that makes him valuable. Isn't that the whole point of this book? Doesn't that make up for a multitude of 1960s-era cultural qualms?

It's close . . . but no cigar.

Here's why: Rudolph is a weirdo whose value is entirely predicated on his perceived usefulness.

In other words, Rudolph's weirdness is commended only once it's deemed useful to Santa and his team. When Santa realizes that he can't make it around the world through the thick fog caused by a horrible blizzard, the idea dawns on him that Rudolph's light alone can get him out of this jam. Up until that very point, however, it's considered a defect, a blemish, a nuisance to be discarded rather than a quality to be cultivated. I wonder how much brighter Rudolph's nose would have glowed on that fateful Christmas Eve had its light been fostered and fed the minute it was identified.

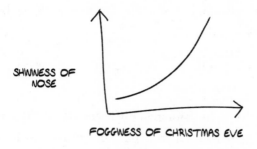

SHINNESS OF NOSE

FOGGNESS OF CHRISTMAS EVE

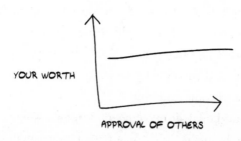

YOUR WORTH

APPROVAL OF OTHERS

That's not the message I want my daughter to grow up believing. That's not the message of the manger or the light it shines as well. The Sacred Weird isn't there in our soul to be exploited. It's not something that's tethered to someone else's opinion. It doesn't have to conform to a pattern or bargain for its worth. It's the undeniable, unshakable reality that is you. It's your journey, complete with all its wrong turns and missteps, the times you've felt pulled and pushed, the times that have felt like an effortless glide, and the seasons when every step felt like slogging through the mud.

You don't have to wait until your life normals out to belong—normal is a construct for small puppets. Real life is weird.

* * *

Lately I've been writing on my friend Mama Moo's farm. Her real name is Lynn, but she introduces herself as Mama Moo since that's what her grandkids call her.

I met Mama Moo at church. I had heard her name around, so once I finally matched a face to her peculiar moniker, I decided I would introduce myself, my wife, and my daughter. With the split-second motility of a ninja, she loaded all our arms up with an assortment of duck, chicken, and turkey eggs from her farm and told us we just had to come and visit.

She and my wife exchanged numbers. A few days later, I came home to tales of an afternoon spent with our daughter on Mama Moo's farm feeding chickens, studying bees, and picking tomatoes, all while literally stopping along the way to smell the flowers—the ones that line her entire property.

So when I began itching for a quiet space to clear my head and chip away a little more at this book, I wondered if it wouldn't appear too crazy to ask Mama Moo after church one Sunday if I could perhaps bum a spot on her porch for a day or two.

When I arrived, I was instantly greeted by two dogs, five or six cows, colors and smells my eyes and ears received like an old flame, and, of course, Mama Moo.

Lynn bought the farm at sixty-four years old. That's not an aging joke, by the way. She literally purchased a sizable piece of workable farming property. Instead of withering to a halt, Lynn, who'd been without a husband for quite some time, decided to make good on a strange dream she'd had since childhood and purchased twenty-four acres of fertile, tillable farmland.

You'll find her out there every morning in rhythm with the sun's song, working away, her pale face slightly veiled by a thick white mask of SPF 30. She sings. She listens. In the quiet moments in between, she marries the two with prayer. She sows. She harvests. She shares.

Gosh, does she share. She delivers food to local restaurants and markets and anyone who even hints at wanting to get in on the goodness. She scolded me the first day I left for not taking enough home with me. The entire farm is one big laboratory, one giant experiment to see just how much wonder can be produced naturally and organically without any of our additives or attempts to manufacture it.

Not wanting to be scolded again, the second day I came ready. Before I left I walked through the garden, bucket in hand, picking fresh parsley, bell peppers, Japanese eggplant, oregano, squash, tomatoes, and black-eyed peas—on top of two fresh cartons of eggs from a variety of resident birds.

To be honest, I was feeling a little disappointed. Not at the produce, but because the reason I'd come to the farm in the first place was to be inspired, and I was leaving after my second day there without any major epiphany.

Mama Moo kept saying, "Everything here is a metaphor for the way the Spirit works."

I kept searching for metaphors, but all I got was a bucketful of vegetables and about two dozen bird embryos I was internally assessing for fat content.

As I wove my way through the colorful rows, just moments before I planned to leave for a meeting I was already late for, Mama Moo cried out, "Look! Come over here and look!"

I made my way over toward the center of the garden, where she was bent over looking at a tomato leaf.

"Do you know what these are?!" she exclaimed.

Tomato leaves, I thought to myself, not really sure what the profound revelation was.

I peered closer at the leaf she was carefully palming to discover a colorful creature resting peacefully on it.

It was bright lime green with brilliant pops of yellow and jet black. I stood there, all of a sudden arrested by both its complexity and its beauty.

"This is the caterpillar that turns into a monarch butterfly," she said. "Isn't it beautiful?"

There was no need to debate this question, no time required to mull it over. The answer was an instinctual and involuntary "Of course."

There it was. The revelation. The metaphor of the Spirit.

All my life (like you, I'm assuming) I've been told the narrative of the ugly caterpillar who one day turns into a beautiful butterfly. Like Rudolph, it's a narrative that assumes that one's value is based on other people's perception, that their good opinion is something to be achieved and treasured.

But this three-inch creature, this small, seemingly insignificant, plump, green structure, complete with heart, brains, eyes, and skin, broke through my thirty-plus years' worth of false notions simply by existing, by doing what it was designed to do—quite possibly before ever knowing what it was destined for.

I'm sure there will be times as my daughter grows up when she doesn't feel beautiful, when she's made fun of or put down for not measuring up to someone else's perception of value. I still vividly remember getting picked on relentlessly for being short and scrawny all throughout grade school. It comes with the territory of being created uniquely. The temptation will be to tell her the narrative of the caterpillar, that one day things will turn out differently, that the facets that make her feel insecure now will someday fall away in a miraculous instant of metamorphosis.

But the problem is that I'm thirty-two years old and I'm still short and scrawny. In the seasons when I lift weights, I tell people that I'm working my way up to normal. These are the genetics I've been handed, the cards I've been dealt.

None of us are promised the future of becoming a butterfly; we are promised the wonder of being a caterpillar.

If my daughter is told to wait for a moment in time when her worth will be transparent to all, she will miss out on the greater reality that her worth is not only present, but abundant and overflowing right now. As with all of us, the shape of her weirdness doesn't have to fit into other people's patterns. She doesn't have to wait to be wonder-full. She doesn't have to believe the myth of the caterpillar.

No one does. No matter what age you are. No matter how weird or normal you feel.

Yes, metamorphosis is miraculous. The cocoon is a catalyst for change (insight rarely, if ever, comes without solitude). But metamorphosis is a process meant for you, not a mandate from others. Your weirdness is a gift in the present tense.

The first thing I recognized when I visited Mama Moo's farm was the amount of land she had. Though much of it was cultivated and cared for, there were still vast amounts of acreage left undeveloped. That didn't stop the sixtysomething-year-old from telling me her vision for those spots, though. Every acre is accounted for in her imagination.

My linear, slightly anxious brain couldn't help but ask, "How do you chip away each day, little bit by little bit, knowing there is so much to do until it's all completed?"

She just echoed what she'd been saying since I got there: "Everything here is a metaphor for the way the Spirit works."

The fact that the farm is still technically unfinished doesn't prevent it from being a gift to anyone who sets foot on its soil (and even those beyond). The fact that there's still a greater metamorphosis to undergo doesn't prevent the tomato plants from producing tomatoes, the chickens from laying eggs, or the flowers from blooming in their brilliant colors.

Thankfully, the value it creates isn't up to us. It's none of our business whether we consider it ready or not. It gives life because the farmer saw it fit that it should, knowing in the back of her mind that there is more to be done.

Take a cue from Mama Moo. Don't fall into the trap that says you should board up your windows until you're ready for the grand opening. You might recognize too late you've been building something for an audience that needed to see your process more than taste your perfection.

There is no sadder lie than the lie that your value is contingent on the opinion of others. If that were the case, Wonka would have manufactured canned soup, Christ would have told safer stories, and Martin Luther King Jr. might have quit while stuck inside a Birmingham jail. To King, the "creatively maladjusted," the imaginative nonconforming weirdos among us, are the ones who pull others toward the future they conceive, not the other way around.

If you came into this book feeling "creatively maladjusted" but not quite sure why, by now I hope you're convinced that you are indeed weird for a reason, that there is a method to your madness, that something in your humanity calls out to a force beyond your complete understanding, and calls you set apart amid a sea of Same.

And yet you're not weird in order to stockpile attention or store up conceit. Rather, when we recognize that every soul comes preinstalled with unique worth, that every human is designed with a divine imagination, we discover the playing field has been leveled.

Yes, we're weird, but we're not weirder than anyone else. And if that's the case, we must tell the others!

They have to know that, like us, everyone has the opportunity to step into the unique shape of their soul, the curious cavern where their deepest purpose and passions lie.

Like us, everyone gets an invitation to belong in a world that would rather they buy in.

Like us, they get to leave Misfits Anonymous and join Misfits Unanimous!

Part 2

What to Make of Your Weirdness

Chapter 7

Manual Labor

Do you wish to rise? Begin by descend-
ing. You plan a tower that will pierce
the clouds? Lay first the foundation of
humility.

—Saint Augustine

I had a fight with my wife last night.

I married Kelly because her capacity to love another
human being stretches far beyond the breadth of any normal person's. I met her in Old Towne Orange, a small

neighborhood in Southern California locked tightly in the year 1964 (judging partly by the fact that they proudly kept the *e* in *Towne* on all modern signage). Amid a region full of new stucco, IKEAs, and silicon everything, Old Towne Orange is this little oasis full of hundred-year-old brick buildings, Frank Lloyd Wright–style craftsman homes, men tinkering on their vintage Chevys and Fords in their driveways, a soda parlor, and the most sincere vinyl record shop you've ever been in, called Mr. C's, after its owner. If you're a fan of the movie *That Thing You Do!*, it's where they filmed many of its exterior shots, a perfect location for a story about local life in the 1960s.

Kelly and I met on a front porch in that town, a symbolic location considering the amount of people we would invite and gather into our home over the next few years.

Kelly and I were both highly motivated and inspired by the idea of loving our neighbor and spent hours conceiving and creating ways to invest in people who were different from us and who, at the same time, shared our neighborhood. It's a big part of what drew us together. After we got married, we hosted parties, turned our little three-hundred-square-foot living room into a symposium for local artists and musicians, and orchestrated neighborhood dinners where everyone was welcome. Homeless people. Struggling families. Wanderers. Misfits.

Our little neighborhood became the vibrant community we had hoped for, where strangers became friends and eventually felt like family, the kind that practices deep, abiding, sticky love even in times of suffering. But, perhaps unsurprisingly to you, this lifestyle wasn't without its challenges.

There was the shifty friend of the homeless lady who showed up at one of our 1950s-themed parties and who, when I asked who he was, replied that his name was Manuel...Manuel Labor. Let me tell you something: it is very hard to kick someone out of your home and look intimidating while wearing a bright-green cardigan, bow tie, and vintage Coke-bottle glasses.

Then there was the group of young girls who caught wind of a house concert we were hosting and proceeded to use our matchbook of a bathroom to have a cocaine fix.

And then there were Jack and Megan.

Jack and Megan lived in a trailer. They had a pet possum they'd found in their backyard. They were bohemian drifters with an uncanny talent for karaoke and missing social cues. I did not like Jack and Megan. Particularly, I didn't like Jack. It didn't matter what we were hosting, Jack and Megan would show up, stay long after everyone had left, and refuse to lift a finger to help clean up, all the while telling awkward jokes and making things miserable. One time they even parked their trailer outside our house so they could drink as much as they wanted and simply crash afterward. Jack was the real-life Cousin Eddie from *National Lampoon's Vacation*. Except, unlike Chevy Chase, I wasn't related to him, not even by marriage. I was under no cultural obligation to like this human being, let alone welcome him into my home.

I'll never forget the time Kelly and I were busy cleaning up from one of our house gatherings. It was late, probably one o'clock in the morning. No one was left except for, you guessed it, our dynamic duo. Drunk and obnoxious, Jack made snarky comments about my wife while she and I scrubbed plates, rearranged furniture, and swept the floor.

And then it happened. As I swept, for no apparent reason, he grabbed an uneaten dinner roll from the not-yet-cleared table and threw it at me, hitting me in the chest.

It took everything in me not to deck the guy clean in the face, chewing him out while I did. Instead I threw down the broom, muttered under my breath, and walked outside to cool off, slamming the door behind me.

The reason Kelly and I got into a fight last night had to do with Jack and Megan, even though it's been years since we've seen either of them. We've since moved to Franklin, Tennessee, and live in a secluded little suburb community. Our life doesn't look the way it did during those glory days of community when we prided ourselves on practicing the "art of neighborhood." It's quieter, more scheduled, and more introverted.

I had brought up Jack and Megan, the fact that they once brought their pet possum to a gathering, the fact that he had once thrown a dinner roll at me at one o'clock in the morning, and the fact that they were awkward, strange, and inconvenient. I was growing more sarcastic, more condescending—and Kelly wasn't having it. She was becoming indignant, welling up with the kind of righteous anger I've seen every once in a while that lets me know I've crossed the line.

Kelly, whom I often liken to one of those statues of Saint Francis that all the animals cling to, has this supernatural ability to care for an unending population of misfits, weirdos, and awkward people who naturally seem to find her.

She looked at Jack and Megan differently. Not as a project and not as a burden, but as two human beings created with *qodesh*, on a search for belonging and a love that wouldn't quit on them.

Eventually Jack left Megan. Shortly after, Megan got into a major car accident. It was Kelly who visited her in the hospital, not just once but daily, spending time with her and her family as she slowly recovered. Kelly kept opening new kinds of doors, entering deeper, more deliberate rooms.

I had slammed mine shut a long time ago.

It's still hard for me to like Jack and Megan, but I've learned to love my wife's weirdness: her capacity to love another human being that stretches far beyond what is normal. I've learned to love the unearthly, sacred superpower she has to actively and perpetually care for those whom most of us would write off as unlovable.

My wife is comfortable with her weirdness. She's at home with her unearthly ritual, the constant stretching of her patchwork quilt over a hill where black sheep gather to eat shepherd's pie. She knows it's not normal. But she knows it's who she is. She's shown me, perhaps more than anyone else, that the further you dive into your weirdness, the greater your capacity grows to love others.

One of the challenges I inevitably had to face,

especially when choosing to write a book about weirdness, is coming to terms with the truth that weird is often inconvenient.

There's the good weird, the kind that creates great art, starts innovative businesses, and moves the world forward—and then there's the kind of weird we'd rather do without, the unrefined and marginalized "strange" we don't know what to do with when we brush up against it in others, the kind we feel justified for belittling and disowning.

The problem is, we can't take one kind without the other.

Weirdness is a spectrum, a continuum on which we could plot flavors ranging from chocolate peanut butter all the way to spinach licorice. We're conditioned from childhood not to understand someone else's weirdness when it contradicts our predetermined patterns. To make matters worse, we live in a world where most people have never been taught what to make of their weirdness. As a result they often express the feeling they feel when they don't belong in ways that potentially harm themselves and others, actions that are usually far worse than hurling a dinner roll at someone.

I stand by the idea that when our lives, schools, companies, and communities choose weirdness, they learn, grow, and thrive. However, if we are going to make space for our own weirdness, it only seems fair that we make peace with those we instinctively push to the margins.

How I wish Christ's simple prayer said, "As you've forgiven us, help us forgive those who trespass against us" or better yet, "Forgive us, and help us forgive others." But it says neither. Instead it says, "Forgive us as we forgive those who trespass against us."[xv]

That's it. No more. No less.

Christ's words imply that the most we should expect from the Divine is to be pardoned to whatever degree we've chosen to extend grace to others.

The *Tao Te Ching* says something similar:

> *When bitter enemies make peace,*
> *Surely some bitterness remains.*
> *How can this be solved?*
>
> *Therefore:*
> *The sage honors his part of the settlement,*
> *But does not exact his due from others.*
> *The virtuous carry out the settlement,*
> *But those without virtue pursue their claims.*
>
> *Heaven's Way gives no favors.*
> *It always remains with good people.*[xvi]

It seems we experience "on earth as it is in heaven," or what Martin Luther King Jr. called "beloved community," only when we make room for the Sacred Weird in others as much as we hope others will make room for it in us.

Chapter 8

Seeds

What you leave behind is not what is
engraved in stone monuments, but what
is woven into the lives of others.

—Pericles

Once upon a time, in the eighteenth century, people used pineapples to judge another person's worth. It cost about $6,500 to grow a pineapple in your home (a hefty amount for anyone), so folks would often display one on their mantel for months at a time while it slowly rotted away. Hosting a party but don't have the cash to throw down on your very own pineapple? Not a problem. You could literally display the fruit of your nonexistent wealth by renting one by the day for just such an occasion.

Once upon a time, in the nineteenth century, people blackened their teeth as a sign of wealth. Sugar was a commodity so rare and expensive that people would paint their teeth black to imply they could afford to delight in the sweet substance so often that their teeth had rotted.[xvii]

Once upon a time, in the twenty-first century, people judged someone's worth by how many "likes" their "selfie" got. A selfie was a photo someone would take of themselves, often angled and edited to make them look better than they did in real life. Whenever someone would post their selfie to the internet, others would judge it by deciding whether or not to press a small button underneath it indicating their approval of said photo. The more people pressed this button showing that they "liked" the photo, the more valuable the person posting it could consider themselves.

It appears our value system is simply a moving target of wildly subjective metrics that changes at least every hundred years or so (this is a conservative number considering the rapid rate of technology and population growth facing our current society). No one is now remembered positively for displaying a rotten pineapple on their mantel. We don't swoon over so-and-so for their display of blackened teeth.

It seems we're prone to confuse influence with idolatry.

If the words of the Presbyterian minister Frederick Buechner is correct, "Idolatry is the practice of ascribing absolute value to things of relative worth."[xviii]

If the measurement of worth is in constant and often ridiculous flux, what should we make of our weirdness? What are we to do with this unique imprinting designed to help others and usher in the future we imagine? What do success, influence, and impact look like in a moment in history when worth is most commonly measured in quantities like followers and likes?

A recent study conducted by the American Sociological Association found that in some cases, the larger your audience is, the less likely it is that they'll do what you ask them to.[xix] This begs the question of whether influence is always about larger numbers and linear growth or if there's a deeper metric worth exploring.

Well, here's a weird idea for you to ponder: Perhaps influence isn't always about multiplication. Perhaps, more often, influence is about division.

True and abiding influence often looks like dividing ourselves (our knowledge, our time, our weirdness) among those within our reach.

If you've ever wondered what a seed's purpose in life is, you've found the right book. I am here to tell you that after a not-so-extensive internet search, I can say with some legitimate pseudoscientific authority that a seed has one singular, specific purpose in life, and that is to pass its genetic information on to the next generation.

That's it.

You'll never witness a seed having an existential crisis

or taking a personality test, because it's never wavered in knowing why it exists on earth. It's to divide its one-of-a-kind strand of DNA and allow the insects and the birds and the wind to carry it wherever it's intended to land.

I want to be a seed.

I've spent so long trying to be the sun and the soil and the rain…and it's exhausting. I simply want to divide the little time I've been given among those within my reach, wherever I find myself, knowing that's how things take root and grow.

I'd often talk to Bill about this. Bill is hands down the most influential person I know. He's a poet first, a pastor second, and a prophet third (though he might disagree with that particular order). Rather than grasping for attention or success, he chooses to spend his time meeting with weirdos like me, waking up at the crack of dawn, conducting his acts of division from dimly lit corner booths inside coffee shops and breakfast diners. He's like Banksy the street artist. He chooses to influence in the shadows, anonymously and unassumingly. His consistent presence, his quiet, ascetic wisdom, and his deep and patient listening followed by his thoughtful questions are the things to which I owe the health of my marriage, my parenting, and my soul. I'm one of many who can say the same.

We live in different parts of the country now so it's harder to stay in touch. Still, I know I can drop a note to him at any time containing something I'm wrestling through, no matter how much shame, angst, or frustration accompanies it, and he'll respond with a reply that's never phoned in, gracious in its thoughtfulness, and recalibrating in its wisdom.

Here's an exchange I pulled from my archives that specifically relates to this topic of influence. I'll spare you my initial message, but in short, I was struggling with feeling as if I had been dealt a hand of cards that was less than extraordinary, a common quandary in my life that Bill was already patiently aware of. I was thinking about my childhood, how I was picked on so much as a kid, and why somehow that past should entitle me to some extraordinary payoff.

If all the comic books are right, shouldn't I have eventually grown into some kind of ideal superhero mutant? If not, then what was all the bad stuff for? Where was the redemption? The justice? The victory lap? Was it coming soon? Had the opportunity passed?

I realize how ridiculous that sounds, but as I mentioned, Bill was a safe space I could come to when my heart didn't believe what my head knew, when my stubborn soul wouldn't reconcile with reason. I'm not sure if you've ever been there, but I live in that place often. If it weren't for voices like Bill's, I'd be a living, breathing, walking argument, twenty-four hours a day, seven days a week.

If you are like me, I hope these words (which if combined with all his poetic wisdom over the years could fill libraries with remarkable commentary for misfits everywhere) will give you the same perspective on influence that they've given me.

Here was his response to my angsty, honest, cynical inquiry:

Hi, CJ—

Good to hear from you—whenever and for whatever reason!

Sorry we couldn't get together when you were out
last time.

It seems to me that there are a couple of false
starts here—which, if followed to their logical con-
clusion, will inevitably lead you astray.

The first is that all life (gifts, talents, success, resources, whatever) is a zero-sum game—a pie, if you
will, which gets cut and distributed seemingly arbi-
trarily. The result ends up being a sense of inevitable
envy when we compare what we think we have gotten with what we think someone else has gotten.
That is a false start on a number of levels.

First, we have no way of knowing or measuring
the relative value of any given thing/life/soul/
resource/talent/whatever. So, from the get-go we
will end up using a false measuring system—and
then be surprised when we can't get the same result
twice. Second, it assumes a closed universe with an
uninvolved creator who has no creative power left,
anyway. If all you have is what you received thus far,
and that is true for everyone, then maybe the idea
would get some altitude. But that is clearly not the
case.

Who can say—certainly not me—what God
might do with what "little" we think we have as
it is offered up to him? And who can say—pot to

potter—"not this, but this" as a measure of greatness? And who can say that grace is no longer enough—or only just barely? And that there is a limited supply, governed by the standards of Western success models? Clearly it is off from the beginning—no wonder it fails at the end. As soon as we make comparison with others the measure of our lives, the game is over. We have lost. The only standard of measure is your true self—which God alone knows. And which is why every failure is a part of the wonder of becoming—as long as we don't get stuck in "coulda, shoulda, woulda."

So, what about all the "bad stuff"? Nothing gets wasted that is offered up to God. As long, however, as we are unwilling to release it, in the hopes that there will one day be an equalizing payment, redeeming it is in our hands. Not a good prospect.

So, the voice we need to hear is that of the Divine—regardless of the other lying or truthing voices we hear, his is the singular priority. And he has spoken regarding you. You are His beloved, chosen and precious, in whom he delights. There is nothing you can do about it.

Except, of course, convince yourself that there must be more. Truth is, if his voice isn't enough, nothing else will be. And if his is—nothing else need be.

There is probably more—but that is enough for now.

—Bill

There's always more with Bill. But that's another wonderful thing about him. He instinctively knows when he's done his job of moving you to tears after you've read a few of his paragraphs, and knows when it's time to stop and just let you reflect for a while.

I desperately long for the kind of influence Bill describes, the kind he embodies early in the morning in those darkened coffee shop corners.

Back when he sent me that note, I still wasn't convinced. It sent me on a journey, a quixotic quest to see if this equation for influence could really be trusted.

What I found was astonishing. This kind of influence, the kind that pollinates and divides itself more than grasping for more, isn't just a nice thought, or a personal feel-good mantra; it's a legitimate and sustainable strategy. While others are seeking accolades, real influencers are busy trying to get into the Small of Fame.

A few examples:

Several years ago, Spotify, the fastest-growing music streaming service in the world, decided it didn't want a bunch of taskmasters on its team, but instead desired a culture of servant leaders. It divided its organization into groups called "squads," small, specialized teams made up of no more than eight team members. At the center of each squad is a leader or "squad coach." A squad coach's job is to do things like mentor, teach, gather people together, and, my favorite, sow seeds.[xx]

Let's travel back even further, to the civil rights movement. Most of us know of heroes like Martin Luther

King Jr. and Rosa Parks, but there's one name most people haven't heard, James Lawson.

In the 1960s, in my town of Nashville, Tennessee, there was a demonstration called the Nashville sit-ins that young black students came up with. They would sit down at prominent whites-only lunch counters all over the city in peaceful opposition to a segregated society. While onlookers hurled insults, threats, and even physical objects, these brave students (kids, really) sat composed, resolute, and peaceful, eventually causing the desegregation of six downtown establishments.

I'm not sure if I could say I had control over any one emotion when I was in college, and here were these students conducting themselves with an unearthly wisdom and authority at the risk of their very lives.

It was James Lawson who taught them how to do that. James would gather students from different colleges around Nashville and pull together workshops, trainings, or squads, if you will, teaching them the ways of Mahatma Gandhi and the principles of nonviolence. He facilitated role-playing games with them, predicting the insults, threats, and assaults they would each face. He was like Mickey Goldmill to Rocky Balboa...except these fighters wouldn't be punching back, at least not literally. Those who attended his trainings included people who went on to be prominent civil rights leaders, like Marion Barry, James Bevel, and John Lewis.

Shortly after the sit-ins took place, James was expelled from Vanderbilt for his work in organizing the demonstration.[xxi]

I found a video made by a local Tennessee newspaper outlet in which, decades later, he's interviewed about his expulsion. The sound is so faint you can barely make out what his still, meek voice is saying:

> Did it take time…to forgive them? No, we didn't even consider anger [or retaliation]. We were not angry… we were people who felt we were trying to follow Jesus….Love and obedience and faithfulness….We were aware because of our faith that you can get crucified and battered if you tried to follow that standard.[xxii]

That's the sound of true influence. The faint but steady sound of a force that doesn't grab or barter but scatters its truth, well aware that the rain will come.

You may never have heard of James Lawson, but his influence is a seed so deeply planted, its roots so tightly gripping the soil, eternity itself couldn't pluck it out.

Next consider Scott and Joel. Scott and Joel are two brothers who play music together. They formed a band called PawnShop Kings and have played everywhere from living rooms to stadiums over the past ten years. What amazes me about their performance is their ability to hush a crowd no matter the venue.

I learned how to quiet down audiences from watching Animal on *The Muppet Show*. If the audience wasn't paying attention to something Kermit was saying, Animal would walk on camera, open his Muppet mouth wide, and shout from the top of his lungs, "QUIET!" Suddenly you would be able to hear a pin drop.

But Scott and Joel take a different approach to getting a crowd's attention. They step away from the mic.

No matter how many loud bands have gone on before them, no matter how many decibels the sound system can handle, Scott and Joel have figured out the best way to command an audience's attention is to be quiet, to permit everything else to fade away and let their two voices intertwine the same way you'd want them to if they were singing in your living room.

I've seen it work time and time again. It would always take a few seconds, but like a disciple witnessing a miracle, I'd notice the shouting and the sound of ice cubes clinking back and forth would eventually subside as all eyes and ears found themselves fixed on the two brothers. Scott and Joel understand that there's a difference between forcing a crowd to listen and inviting it. They choose to go small in an environment where everyone else is busy trying to multiply their sound. And they win every time.

One last story about influence: I remember sitting down one night with Kelly and admitting to her that most days I wake up feeling I have something to prove to the world, how this problem seems unshakable, a weight chained to my ankle that only gets heavier with each passing season. She looked at me with a calm, earnest glimmer in her eye, the kind that first drew me to her, the kind that will still shine just as strong once the rest of her has faded and folded, and asked, "What if you changed your perspective from having something to prove to having something to give?"

SOMETHING TO PROVE

SOMETHING TO GIVE

In that mundane, painfully ordinary moment, while I was sitting on the couch in our living room, truth came crashing into me through this strange and profound little thought.

Something to give.

It's a phrase I write on my hand whenever I'm about to do something that makes me nervous. It's something I let rise to the surface of my soul whenever I'm busy comparing myself to someone else.

Still, regardless of Bill's words, regardless of Kelly's challenge, regardless of all the research and data I collected out there, this idea that influence is more concerned with giving than growing, dividing than multiplying is something I honestly didn't believe fully until a short time ago.

A few months back, Kelly had a miscarriage. It was early on, within the first few weeks of the pregnancy, weeks during which we felt as if we were constantly holding our breath, knowing how often these things happen.

That still didn't take the sting away from sitting in that cold room during what was supposed to be our baby's first ultrasound, peering deeply into that monitor and seeing nothing. I remembered back to the first time we saw our older child's little embryo zipping all over the womb, doing backflips and somersaults, her excited, extroverted personality already showing. I was no doctor, but this was clearly different. A few minutes later, a nurse came in and confirmed what Kelly and I both knew in our guts.

I was pretty strong, rationalizing it in my mind, and, as most men would, thinking practically about our next steps. Then the nurse said something that for some reason made it more personal. She said, "It looks like something happened around the fifth or sixth week that caused the baby to stop growing, caused its heart to stop."

That was my kid. Nobody messes with my kid. The idea that something had overpowered my child, a part of who I am, made me want to speak to that little seed like a football coach. I wanted to yell at the top of my lungs in that doctor's office, "Come on, buddy! You can make it!"

But I knew the fight was already over.

That's when I stopped rationalizing.

That's when I stopped preparing.

That's when the tears started to fall.

Kelly was convinced it was a boy from the moment she found out she was pregnant, and, without my knowledge, started thinking of names. At one point she came across the name Leo, which means "brave like a lion." She didn't think I'd like it, so she kept it to herself, but the name kept circling around her head, almost haunting her. After finding out about the miscarriage, Kelly named our brave little fighter Leo. I love the name. I think it suits him.

I've heard over and over again how no one ever talks about miscarriages and how common they are, how it rocks some families to their core. I'm being honest when

I say Kelly and I both felt blessed to walk into our second pregnancy with the awareness that this kind of thing happens more often than most people talk about. We took stock of our grief and acknowledged that we were surrounded by friends and family who genuinely loved us and had dropped whatever they were doing to support and comfort. We both spoke of the many other blessings we could easily point to that made us rich beyond earthly measure.

I felt as if I was handling this setback in stride. I wasn't hiding from my grief. I wasn't spinning out of control either.

But the story didn't end just because I was ready to turn the page.

Kelly is a collector. I'm a purger. The show *Hoarders* gives me nightmares. I'll donate a shirt I haven't worn in six months, delete something off the internet I'm no longer proud of, or cut off a relationship with someone I feel has wronged me. I have a sometimes toxic tendency to move on from things quickly, especially when they sting.

I felt I had done my job in grieving Leo. I was ready to count the loss and place it deep into the archives of my memory, pulling it out only every so often as a potential comfort to some other couple going through a similar situation.

I didn't know Leo wasn't done influencing people.

My mother-in-law, Jeanie, is a self-proclaimed eccentric, no stranger to all things weird. She's a painter, a singer, and a collector of people, objects, and ideas that are just slightly off the beaten path. I've come to love the fact that whenever we visit her, we ought to come expecting the unexpected, wondering what wacky new piece of artwork we'll be introduced to, what color she'll have painted her dining room table, or what old hymn she's arranged into a modern smooth jazz cover on her keyboard. The bossa nova version of "Blessed Assurance" is my favorite.

Kelly decided to share the name she'd given our baby with Jeanie, the way I hope our daughter will one day share little window openings into her soul with Kelly.

Jeanie faithfully volunteers at a rehab program for young men convicted of minor drug crimes. As an alternative to prison, these men often enter this program in a last-ditch effort to get clean and turn their lives around. Jeanie leads music on the weekends for these tough and hardened offenders, swooping in with her portable keyboard and tambourine and providing them all with a healthy dose of everyone's favorite antidote to a lifestyle of drugs and minor theft . . . Christian jazz.

A few weekends ago, during her regular routine, Jeanie paused to share some words Kelly had written about Leo and our journey of letting him go with this group of troubled young men. A few days after, she wrote this letter describing what happened next:

Leo,

I shared your mother's writing of your life and passing with others struggling in their own way today. I acknowledged that you were wanted by both your mama and dad, something often missing in families today. I shared that being unwanted makes us struggle in ways we seldom understand. I saw some resonating nods and a few dropped heads.

One quiet young man approached me at the end to tell me he had recently returned to drugs after his mother had told him she NEVER wanted him. Something I'm sure he felt most of his life by the weeping punctuating his story. My arms drew him in and I could feel his sobs shaking us both.

When he was finally able to compose himself he expressed how much it had meant to him that I had shared about you today. As he turned to leave, I asked his name. "Leo," he said. "My name is Leo!"

Influence doesn't always look like something growing. Sometimes it looks quite small. Sometimes it looks broken, forgotten, even dead. In my foolishness I believed Leo's influence was over because I'd resolved it in my mind. Little did I know that it wasn't up to me. I don't think I've ever felt more small and yet so seen in my whole life.

The parts of your life you deem fragmented, overlooked, outlawed, and lifeless might be the very components the Divine uses to move our world toward wholeness.

I now know what the weeping willow knows, whose mighty tears provide shade and comfort. I now understand what the moth understands who can't help but seek the light after shedding his grave clothes. I now realize how a lion can roar without ever making a sound.

Influence happens when we realize our life counts rather than spending our life counting.

Chapter 9

Farmers in a World of Hunters

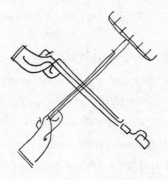

Put your faith in the two inches of
humus
that will build under the trees
every thousand years....
Practice resurrection.
—Wendell Berry

Every seed is also a farmer, scattering itself over the soil, stimulating revival, and joining in the good work of feeding those who are empty.

I once heard a story[xxiii] about a woman in Ireland who was born with dwarfism. While she had come to expect negative attention the way she expected the sun to rise and fall on any given day, as you might imagine her soul never quite got used to it. While sticks and stones leave marks, so do stares and snickers. At about eleven or twelve years old, she was met with an opportunity to undergo a surgery that would stretch out her bones, giving her about another six inches of height. At the age at which I was busy doing anything and everything to assimilate to my surroundings, after thinking about it long and hard, she decided to refuse the procedure. Instead she chose to remain different at the very point Same offered an ultimatum, promising her everything it had to offer.

Today she enjoys a career as a middle school teacher. Because of her uncommon shape, she possesses an equally uncommon ability to navigate situations in which a child is made fun of. When one boy picked on another, calling him "a weirdo" in front of the class, she asked if she herself should be picked on too since "weird" meant "different" and she was clearly different from most. The boy, who loved her, said of course not, and apologized to the other student for his hurtful words.

It's quite fascinating, isn't it? Had this beautiful creature taken the necessary measures to eradicate her weirdness early on, she might never have had access to its healing power.

Our weirdness may not be as visible as it is for others, we may not wear it on our sleeve or bear it on our body, but each one of us carries a peculiar piece of divine worth.

What a strange paradox it is that those qualities we possess, the ones that have the power to heal and bless and change the earth around us, are usually the very traits we're tempted to rid ourselves of.

This presents us with an inevitable fork in the road. We can choose to join the crowd of voices demanding we fit in or else. We can spend our lives trying to surgically eliminate the weirdness in our bones. Or we can cultivate the blessings it provides. We can become farmers in a world of hunters. We can choose to go around planting seeds instead of firing bullets at the miraculous that so often gets labeled as "mistaken."

While we can attempt to kill off weirdness with the swift pull of a trigger, farming, on the other hand, takes careful time. It's slow, abiding work fixed on nourishing small things that are buried deep, bringing them to breath.

This, we know, is the best kind of work. While the hare was busy sprinting and hyping, it seems the tortoise never cared to hustle. I don't think he was even out to win. I think he just didn't want to miss the scenery. As we all know, the tortoise eventually went on to beat the hare. The reason is not a mystery. He simply remained faithful to what the great Creator endowed him with. He somehow learned to keep going even when the scenery changed or his stout appendages got tired, or his shell overheated for the thousandth time. While the hare was busy showing off, quietly and methodically a misfit was creating movement.

When we busy ourselves hunting down the wild weird inside us, it's ultimately a losing battle. The good news is that the Sacred Weird cannot be killed. It cannot be eliminated. It can only be covered, masked, renounced, and ignored. It can be left for dead, but it will not die. It will wait patiently behind stone until it is resuscitated, resurrected, and blooming.

I want to throw my hands into the clay where I am planted, the soil I am bound to return to one way or another. I want to carve past the stiff, lifeless boxes of my own self-preservation and make room for a field, an ever-stretching thicket of plants and trees and wildflowers all ripe with their own colors and textures for the sharing.

I want to fight to stay weird in a world that needs to be woken up, to act upon the mysterious truth that whatever makes me different cultivates the difference I'm bound to make.

Chapter 10

The Shame of Same

There's a place in the soul where you've
never been wounded.

—Meister Eckhart

Tim was my hero. In college I wanted to be just like
him. He was about fifteen years older than I and
led a successful nonprofit organization. I spent as much
time as I could studying his leadership style and cher-
ished the few moments throughout my college career
when he cleared his schedule to meet with me. I told

him to hold nothing back, look for flaws, and coach me on how to become a better communicator.

About a year after I graduated college, Tim noticed some interesting things I was creating and suggested to his organization's communications director that I come in for an interview.

A few weeks later I found myself working alongside about sixty other employees of this thriving organization led by the very person I had been taking cues from for years. I was barely twenty-three years old and feeling as if I had "arrived" in life…a naive notion only a twenty-three-year-old could hold.

It didn't take long, however, to discover that the culture was disorganized, the expectations were unclear, and Tim's vision was completely all over the place. I spent most of my time there unsure of what I was supposed to do, how I was supposed to do it, and, worst of all, why it even mattered.

If my fragile, real world–averse ego wasn't already on the brink of total existential combustion, what happened next was like pouring lighter fluid on it.

My direct report, the communications director Tim had suggested should hire me, called me into her office to tell me that it didn't seem I was fitting into their culture. "You ask a lot of questions," she told me.

That was the beginning of the end…which is funny, because the actual beginning wasn't very long in the first place. I think I worked there for a total of eight months at best before I quit, just a few weeks before they would have fired me, I'm convinced.

During that time I was afforded a grand total of two to three personal interactions with Tim, who was always off traveling somewhere or too busy to be involved in a project I was trying to get off the ground.

A few qualifiers before I press on any further. First, I understand that if you're running a sixty-person organization you're not expected to spend ample time with every employee, especially some twenty-three-year-old punk kid who thinks he knows everything. However, I will submit to the jury the fact that I was brought in specifically to help Tim and his VP connect more with their donors through media. Part of my job was to spend time with the guy. If he couldn't give up any of his schedule to dialogue, produce, and collaborate, I literally couldn't do my job.

Second, I'm a firm believer that everyone needs a good workplace debacle in their lives. Everyone should experience at least one job they leave thinking, *Well, that experience was definitely not for me. I am clearly not what they were looking for, and they are clearly not what I want either.*

At some point everyone needs a clean black eye and a busted nose to remind them that there are some situations in life you should stay away from unless they're worth fighting over.

The earlier the better.

The final fantastic blow came on the day before I left the organization for good. During my brief tenure there, I was quick to place blame for all the lack of cooperation, direction, and vision I experienced at the organization on my direct report. She was my scapegoat, a muse for my cynicism and self-righteousness. She was an easy target.

She was constantly stressed, her slender frame always hunched over as if every meeting she came from had beaten the backbone out of her.

I was too naive to notice that was exactly what was happening. Tim was the one she was always in meetings with. Tim was the one giving her direction (or not). Tim was the one responsible for setting the vision. Tim had been the one who urged her to hire me. Tim, as it turned out, had been the one who urged her to let me go.

The day before I left, a coworker who had been in those meetings, someone who knew my direct report well, took it upon herself, out of pity for either me or her, to tell me who really wanted to cut some "dead weight."

I had been discarded by my hero.

I had put someone on a pedestal, someone who was never really game to reciprocate with any significant energy or investment. I had put my faith in a future that hinged on a personality, and was surprised when I discovered personalities can have disorders.

Tim isn't a villain. To vilify Tim, to paint him as a callous and mean-spirited dictator, would be dishonest and shortsighted. Tim had a direct report too. We all do. Often they're the lying, demanding phantoms who fire off orders inside our own heads.

The communications director I mentioned, my former direct report, who worked under Tim, left the organization a year or two after I did. I've run into her several times over the years and, in doing so, have realized that it's possible for a woman to become younger as she ages.

Her body has straightened. Her wrinkles have faded. There's a glow where she once seemed dim.

As for Tim, it's been years since that job and years since I've seen him. I don't think about that time in my life very often, and I wouldn't say it still weighs on my soul.

A few months ago, however, I saw Tim post a photo on the internet, technology's innovative solution for helping you remember things you'd rather forget. In it he was standing arm in arm between two other leaders, both around my age. Leaders I knew. Guys he'd met around the same time that he'd met me. Underneath the photo, Tim described these men as the men he had chosen to invest in, mentor, and coach over the past decade, adding how proud he'd become of both of them and their accomplishments.

It was a sucker punch from an unfriendly ghost. It's not that Tim didn't care about anyone. He just didn't care about me.

I mean, I had vision! I had talent! I had leadership potential!

To this day I'm not sure why I was overlooked. I'm not sure why I was unaccepted. What did those guys have that I didn't? What was I lacking? Where did I come up short?

We've all felt this way before. It doesn't matter who it was; it might have been a parent, a spouse, a sibling, or a friend. Someone we loved didn't love us back. Someone saw the Sacred Weird spilling out of our soul and instead only wanted to see Same.

Thankfully, it's not up to them. It never has been.

Up until now I've made a case for why weirdness is something that ought to be cultivated and shared versus silenced, shut out, and ignored. But what about the times we *want* to be weird, the moments we truly desire to be the one who brings a unique point of view or insight to the table, but instead remain convinced we're destined for a uniform and flavorless life?

Some of us don't need to be persuaded that Same is the enemy, we're just not sure we have enough weird in us to do anything about it. For us, Same sounds a lot like shame.

I've come to realize that the Sacred Weird lives somewhere deeper than our competitive drive to be original or unique. In the wise words of Thomas Merton, "We have the choice of two identities: the external mask which seems to be real…and the hidden, inner person who seems to us to be nothing, but who can give himself eternally to the truth in whom he subsists."[xxiv]

The Sacred Weird is the representation of our truest self, something that, while capable of being masked, cannot be taken away.

Just because our weirdness is not for everyone doesn't mean it isn't there at all.

C. S. Lewis seemed to build on Merton's thought when he said, "No man who bothers about originality will ever be original: whereas if you simply try to tell the truth (without caring twopence how often it has been told before) you will, nine times out of ten, become original without ever having noticed it."[xxv]

Are all 6.4 billion people who exist on the planet

individually weird? With the vast amount of information traveling at nanosecond speeds and orbiting our daily lives, is there really such a thing as originality anymore? Can we trust our own imaginations and passions, especially when someone else out there seems to be doing it so much better than we can?

The answer to these questions can be found, but not without our first plunging deep down past the outer shell of what we are often quick to call "our story" and into the quiet, consecrated shelter of our identity.

There has been a tremendous emphasis on all things related to "story" in our society over the years. Ad campaigns want you to tell your story, hoping that by doing so, you'll help them tell theirs. Social media encourages us to share our stories, giving the entire world an opportunity to like and react to them with the push of a button. Creative services on their surface, all seem to aim at helping clients tell a compelling story. This is all well and good, but it's all happening in correlation with a culture that's constantly disappointed, anxious, obsessive, and discontented. Perhaps this is because we've made story the be-all and end-all when its intended purpose is to serve as a beginning.

I do not believe your story matters as much as you might have been told.

Your story is not who you are. It's not even a version. It's merely a presentation, an outer fencing, a collection of modules that are easy to manipulate. This is not to say your story isn't powerful. Arguably, it can be given too much power. On one hand, your story can provide others with a window into your true identity. On the other, it has the power to draw the curtains.

Is there truth to your story? Absolutely. Can your story move us and shape us and help us understand what we once couldn't? Of course it can. But even the greatest story succeeds only at illuminating who we are and whom we are becoming. It cannot write those things for us.

Your story is not as important as your identity.[xxvi] It can only hold a candle to it. There's a holy and hallowed place deep in your gut that's uninterested in the shifting tides of comparison and acceptance, a place that's weird and unique and completely you without you ever having to do a thing to keep it that way, because it's been divinely given, not earned, conjured, or finessed. You've felt it before. You've listened to its reassuring whispers accompanying the pounding of your chest. You've followed it with an unlikely courage against all reason and rationale or the warnings of well-meaning friends. You've gotten so swallowed up in its perfect belonging, if just for a moment, that you've forgotten about your status, or your success rate, or how you might be perceived by others. It's who you were before the world told you it didn't matter. It will kindle any story you will ever write because it's been written in you.

Until you're convinced that you are valuable beyond your ability to produce anything, beyond security or success, you will constantly be holding yourself (and others) to a standard that will never satisfy you. It's as if you're trying to measure weight with a ruler or height with a scale.

However, when we press into the astonishing reality

that no one has ever quite flavored the world like us, and no one can…even if they try, we start to recognize that there's enough weird to go around. We stop worrying about competition and suddenly can't wait to collaborate. We stop obsessing about earning, squeezing, and scroogeing our way to the top. Instead we start giving our weirdness away freely, realizing that no matter how much we give, our souls will never run dry. We start looking for opportunities to combine our weirdness with other people's weirdness like mad scientists set loose inside a laboratory of infinite possibilities.

This profound revelation—that your weirdness isn't just for you to bottle up inside, but there to join others, to facilitate belonging in a world where belonging is in short supply—is the first step to discovering exactly what to make of your weirdness.

It took me a while to figure out what to make of mine.

There are literally thousands of books about how to become wildly successful, how to acquire massive amounts of wealth and live the best life imaginable.

This isn't that kind of book. I'm not that kind of writer.

Here, as I approach the middle of my fourth decade on earth, I'm slowly learning what I'm supposed to do with this small speck of dust this spirit gets to embody for a few decades more, if that.

I'm supposed to tell people they're OK.

That might sound lackluster. That may not seem as sexy a promise as the promise of wealth, success, or perpetual happiness. But it's a promise I can keep, and one I believe is more liberating.

For each of us, every new morning comes with a constant barrage of messages, a thick cloud we've been methodically conditioned to trudge through if we're ever going to do something as basic as drive on a highway, visit a grocery store, listen to the radio, or turn on our television.

It's the message that something's missing.

Something's wrong.

And it can be fixed.

You can be better.

And you should.

Unless you're living in the middle of the woods, cut off from any technological breakthrough since the printing press, chances are you find yourself endlessly traveling through a maze of this kind of advertising only occasionally interrupted by real-life interaction devoid of any sale or bargain. Our popular culture has no commercial breaks. Instead it's become up to us to do the breaking.

No wonder we're slogging to the end of the day depressed and full of anxious thoughts. From dawn till dusk we've been wading through one not-so-subliminal message after another telling us that our worth is conditional, our weirdness should be covered, and our defects need curing.

Weirdness often feels painfully lonely until you've realized you've always belonged.

* * *

I sat stuck at a light in my base-model Ford Focus a few years ago on the last warm afternoon before autumn, the sun dipping and backing away as if to say, "Enough is enough."

I cried out to God that I just wanted to be successful. I just wanted to resemble the others who seemed to fill this town with a carefree confidence that everything was taken care of because they had "made it," that they had arrived on some imaginary shore I know now was never really sure to begin with.

I heard an inner voice as clear as the late-summer sky was that afternoon, with a quiet, calm, and resolute assurance: "You're not going to show people how to be successful. You're going to show people that they're OK."

I didn't need any further explanation.

Sitting there in that gray Focus with a dent in the roof because a branch fell on it outside our garageless house, with coffee stains and stale Cheerios stuck to the sun-grayed carpet that was once jet black and smelled like Armor All, I realized I had everything I needed and then some. I had a wife who never vacillated for a second about being up for the adventure of an unconventional life with an unconventional husband who has an unconventional vocation. I had a daughter with ten fingers and ten toes who had taught me that joy comes from collecting things like leaves and twigs and understanding that there's a certain kind of bug whose butt glows in the dark. I became aware of that ancient scripture about birds feasting and humans fussing.

I am OK.

I've stepped into the frigid waters of weird, have chosen not to follow the path of Same, and I'm here to tell you that air miraculously still stretches my lungs until they push it back out in rhythm with the universe. I'm here to tell you that my heart still pumps the blood it's been taught to, that there continues to be a roof over my head and enough food to eat.

You are OK.

You may be miles away from where you're convinced you ought to be. You may be suffering through something harder than I can even imagine. I promise you, you've got what you need to make it through. The strange reality that you still exist in the universe means its author hasn't given up on you. It sees the weird you inhabit and whispers, "Keep going."

I'm learning that it's not only OK to be weird. It's also weird to be OK.

As we drift from the days of our grandfathers, wars fought by drafted men, and houses built by survivors happy just to be alive, it's become a paradigm shift to practice the ancient and forgotten art of contentment. In a "you deserve this," "get it while you can" era, it's strange to pause from the grabbing, the grasping, the pawing, the striving, and the endless quest for more, more, more…and then some. It's weird to revel in the reality of what exists right before us, the untapped but accessible beauty we're so often tempted to overlook.

I'm not suggesting we anesthetize ourselves or relinquish what we're capable of. I'm not saying that we should confuse contentment with complacency. Complacency by definition is unaware of any potential threats or danger. Contentment simply makes friends with the danger.

What I'm saying is all this worry about greatness and preoccupation with power puts us at an imaginary disadvantage we're convinced is real. We've turned chasing both greatness and power into a sport we can never win, instead of embracing them as qualities that are already alive and actively working within us.

The work then is to shift our dreams far away from excess, beyond even comfort, to something deeper and far more satisfying: wholeness. The life-altering idea that our unique journeys are in fact everything we need, that our weirdness is our worth and that our worth isn't contingent upon anyone else's metric, carries all the power and greatness we could ever imagine.

We're not weird so we can make a dent in the universe. The universe doesn't need more dents. The universe needs whole people. It needs people who roam its bruised and crooked terrain understanding the glorious truth that worth doesn't come from an external source to be hunted and captured, but is simply farmed and cultivated from within.

That's how minds begin to change.

That's how communities begin to heal.

That's how movements begin to spark.

Chapter 11

The Gift of Groove

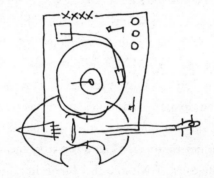

For the loser now will be later to win.
—Bob Dylan, "The Times They Are
A-Changin'"

If you ever come to my house, one of the first things we're going to do is put on a vinyl record. It's one of the things that make me weird, but it's the best way to listen to what an album was supposed to sound like when it was created. You just have to hear it to experience it. Sonically speaking, when you play an MP3, all the quality, the detail, the ghost notes, and the groove have been crunched, squandered, and squeezed into a thin export small enough to fit on your phone. But when you listen to vinyl, you hear it all—the lows, the mids, and the highs all dancing together the way they were meant to. There's space, enough room for the nuance to be heard and appreciated.

When you listen to vinyl, you're not running, you're not driving, you're not shuffling from one song to the next. You're just listening, surrendered to the inconvenience that often accompanies quality. It's a holy experience.

I wish our conversations with each other were more like this. I wish our politics, religious institutions, and schools were less like MP3s and more like vinyl records. I wish we weren't so busy trying to squeeze our point of view into sandpaper sound bites and instead created the space necessary for nuance to make its voice heard, to let the undertones that shape our stories behind the scenes rise up to the surface without the threat that they'll be devalued or ignored.

My friend Evan came over the other day to listen to a new album I had just recently purchased. It was a reissue of Stevie Wonder's hit record *Talking Book*, which he released in 1972, the one with "You Are the Sunshine of My Life" and my favorite, "Superstition," one of his biggest hits.

Evan, a walking encyclopedia of all things music, told me a story about that song, one I haven't been able to get out of my mind since. He said that in the studio, Stevie, at the young age of twenty-two, was trying to communicate what he imagined the drum groove to be. He had hired a professional studio drummer, but no matter how hard that poor guy tried, he just wasn't able to translate what Stevie's imagination wanted to hear whenever the recording lights switched on. So Stevie decided to get behind the kit and record the groove himself. A major plot point to this story worth mentioning: Stevie Wonder wasn't a drummer. He knew just enough to be dangerous and, more importantly, he knew the groove he wanted.

I sat there with my jaw on the floor as Evan relayed this story to me. The particular song was now playing over the speakers. "If you listen closely, the drums are really sloppy," he pointed out to me. "The fills seem a little off and kind of forced." I couldn't believe it. He was right.

I must have listened to "Superstition" hundreds of times throughout my life—the first time I heard it I was probably four or five years old. This was the only time I'd ever noticed all the nuanced imperfections, the sound of a kid who didn't really know the standard rules and practices a studio drummer would normally come into a gig with. The fills *are* sloppy. The high hat is almost childishly simple. The snare hits don't always land perfectly. I spent most of my high school and college days as a drummer, so this was especially shocking.

There's one thing Stevie Wonder's performance has, though: Groove. Groove for days.

I can't tell you how many times I've quit something before I even began because I thought someone else could do it more skillfully than I could. I can't tell you how many times I've hired a professional for a creative project only to realize later that I could have done it better myself. At only twenty-two, Stevie understood what I'm still learning: that it doesn't matter if it's not perfect, it matters if it comes from you.

The bottoms of our oceans are full of strange, remarkable, universe-altering ideas that never made it to shore for fear that they weren't pristine, that they didn't measure up against an invisible and arbitrary grid no one quite seems to have the coordinates to.

Your weirdness, the ideas that come from your own imagination and the rhythms that rumble in your own soul, are everything you need to create what only you can, creations with the capacity to make our world a far more beautiful, interesting place to live. Your weirdness is our gain. Your perfection is our loss.

There's a difference between ignorance and innocence. Ignorance is the unawareness that something better exists. Innocence is the freedom from that unawareness.

Ignorance sticks its fingers in its ears, burrows its head in the sand, and willfully refuses to consider the possibility that we may not know everything, that something or someone out there might outperform, outlast, or outsmart us.

Innocence on the other hand is the natural religion of children, a sacrament we are still invited to partake in as grown-ups, one that liberates us from the shame of being wrong, deficient, or unfinished and releases us from comparison's clenched jaws.

To confuse one with the other is an old and tired

script dating all the way back to the garden, a strategy used by a snake-oil serpent to tempt Eve with the promise of Same.

"Rid yourself of ignorance and be like God," went the familiar sales pitch. In reality, as she hid between bushes under blankets of shame, it was her innocence that seemed to vanish like a vapor.

Our best work is our most innocent work—work drenched in honesty, purity, and present tense. It's exactly who we are, regardless of where we want to be. It's set apart from our ambition, our comparisons, and our desire for validation. It's not birthed from an aim to look like what we admire but out of a centered admiration for the weirdness within ourselves.

I recently caught up with my friend Will, a fantastic children's writer and illustrator. Perhaps more than any other person I know, Will teaches me what it looks like to be oneself. Lately he's been drawing all sorts of cartoons and writing new poems that are truly his best work yet. In an effort to encourage him, I pointed out that he's really seemed to hone in on his unique style. His response was far more encouraging to me than my compliment was to him, which I've come to expect from Will; it's just who he is.

He told me he thinks the reason for this is that he'd finally made peace with his limitations. He had finally acknowledged that his art wasn't going to look the way he once wanted it to, resembling someone else's work. Instead it was going to look like him. His circles aren't going to be perfect. His expressions are going to be simpler than he prefers. His lines more crude than those of other artists out there.

But as someone who's watched his work closely over the years, I can say that it's his imperfect shapes that make his work stand out, his simple expressions that make it relatable, and his carefree lines that give it a childlike wonder. If it weren't for Will's weirdness, we'd never get a front-row seat to that wonder.

And if there's one thing we could use more of in the world, it's wonder. It's astonishment. It's the profound privilege of walking through what the powers of Same consider mundane with the audacity to recognize it as vivid and holy.

> *Earth's crammed with heaven,*
> *And every common bush afire with God:*
> *But only he who sees, takes off his shoes,*
> *The rest sit around it, and pluck blackberries.*
>
> —from *Aurora Leigh*,
> Elizabeth Barrett Browning

We need your weirdness to remind us that there's wonder in a world that often feels cold and pointless. We need your groove to beckon us to dance when we're tempted to run from one thing to the next. Your weirdness is a gift to us, an invitation to take notice of the burning bushes springing up between the cracks in our sidewalks.

* * *

Yesterday I went up to take the Eucharist at church. There are a lot of religious traditions I don't understand, but there's something about taking a piece of bread and a sip of wine that reminds me of the strange truth that my sustenance as well as my joy aren't found in the things I strive for, but gifts I need only stretch out my hands to receive.

As I was walking up with my wife and daughter to receive these gifts, I heard a thin, scratchy sound coming from the east corner, where the musicians collect to play. My first reaction was of honest and, admittedly, slightly annoyed surprise.

We attend a church in Nashville that hosts some of the most incredible musicians in the entire world. The people who usually perform during our church services have written songs that have won Grammys, for goodness' sake! Why was I all of a sudden hearing squeaks and scratches?

As the sound continued, I realized it belonged to a violin. The song it was timidly trying to scrape out? Leonard Cohen's "Hallelujah."

Well, now I had to investigate. This is quite possibly one of the most beautiful songs of the past century, if not all of history. Who was defacing it? And during the Eucharist no less?

Jesus would not be happy.

I glanced over at the musicians' corner and noticed that the violin's player was a girl who couldn't have been more than eleven or twelve years old.

It's quite amazing how quickly our cynicism transforms into empathy once we see a face.

All of a sudden, what my ears had found irritating just seconds ago was now beautiful when paired with what my eyes saw. Here was this child playing the "secret chord," opening a window into the kind of universe this ancient ritual I was about to partake in was symbolizing, a universe where what sounds strange and unfinished is the very thing that pleases the Divine.

Her song was my entire week that led up to that morning. It was all the muddy thoughts and words I wish I could white out, all the misses and "didn't measure up" moments, all the rejection and feelings of failure I brought with me to the table, hands open, mouth open, just trying to scratch out a broken hallelujah.

Her honest, sincere performance truly suggested the supernatural. It was everything she had, uncommonly courageous in a room full of musical experts, echoing Christ's words in the gospel of Saint Matthew:

> At that time the disciples came to Jesus and asked, "Who, then, is the greatest in the kingdom of heaven?"
>
> He called a little child to him, and placed the child among them. And he said: "Truly I tell you, unless you change and become like little children, you will never enter the kingdom of heaven. Therefore, whoever takes the lowly position of this child is the greatest in the kingdom of heaven. And whoever welcomes one such child in my name welcomes me." [xxvii]

Our attempts to live out of our true selves, our Sacred Weird, often seem to present themselves as squeaks and scratches, bruises and blemishes.

But if there's one thing I love about the Eucharist, it's the same thing every kid knows after a long, hard day on the playground: that our scrapes and scars are what make us sacred.

There are no failures to a child who hasn't yet gotten the weird kicked out of her. There are simply experiments, an infinite universe of what-ifs to be explored. She is a glad scientist. Life is a laboratory for her. Her scraped knees and imperfect scribbles are simply evidence of an adventure worth taking, made all the more meaningful because they came with nuggets to learn from.

At some point the very lines of our scribbles change and we start giving those experiments the name I previously mentioned: failures. This new precarious title gives us a convenient excuse to stop asking "What if?" from the vantage point of wonder, and to begin asking the same question from a new angle of anxiety and self-preservation. "What if I can?" slowly morphs into "What if I cannot?" We start shutting down all things weird, unknown, and untested for safe, reliable, and Same.

What if we treated what we perceive as failures to sweep under the rug as experiments to pursue, learn from, and share with others? What if we risked, dared, and imagined with open hands, knowing that the scrapes will come either way, whether we choose to act or not? In this scenario, however, the scrapes eventually heal, making you stronger.

Researcher and statistician Nassim Nicholas Taleb calls this phenomenon *antifragility*. He posits that the opposite of *fragile* isn't *robust*, because while fragile things break when met with disruption, robust things simply remain the same. The true opposite of fragile is *anti*fragile. When something is antifragile, it actually improves when it comes into contact with stress, resistance, and disruption.[xxviii]

For those who partake in the Eucharist, this is the resurrection.

For those willing to experiment, this is what learning feels like.

For those who open up their true selves to rejection, this is the still, small voice that whispers, "It's not up to them."

Our weird scratching and squeaking, our rough sketches and storyboarding, our awkward pauses, and even our total air balls…they're all a hallelujah (or "God be praised").

They're the secret chords that evoke the Sacred Weird and send us into a future where the childish, lowly, and forgotten lost causes, once left for dead, come back to life stronger than anyone could've ever imagined.

Well, any grown-up at least.

Chapter 12

Move toward the Monsters

He was afraid at last. A tremor ran
through him, like a shudder passing over
the sea; but on the sea one shudder follows another till there are hundreds of
them, and Peter felt just the one. Next
moment he was standing erect on the
rock again, with that smile on his face and
a drum beating within him. It was saying,
"To die will be an awfully big adventure."
—J. M. Barrie, *Peter Pan*

I love going to the grocery store. If my wife asks me to go, I'm behind the steering wheel before she can give me the list.

I think it's because even on my worst day, when I'm working on some big project and it's not coming together, or I'm trying to solve a massive problem and just hitting a wall, I can go the grocery store and accomplish something. I realize this is as close as I'm ever going to get to connecting with my primal roots, as I leave the safe confines of my suburban cave, hunt for food in the wild, and bring home to my family the bounty of frozen pizzas and Cap'n Crunch (items not on my wife's list but still clearly important).

I can get lost in a daze of instant gratification set to a soundtrack of soft rock disrupted only by the occasional muffled loudspeaker announcement as I stride slowly back and forth among the aisles, looking for the cure for whatever ails my mangled brain. It's both a sedative and a dopamine rush at the same time.

As a writer, I spend most of my time in the ethereal, the conceptual, and the abstract. It's a long game, much more like Risk than the more instantly satisfying Hungry Hungry Hippos.

No one ever told me that writing often feels a lot like wrestling.

Most days I don't want to wrestle. I don't really want to opt into the kind of work that's weird, vulnerable, mysterious, and uncertain. I don't want to put in the effort to create something that stands out for the world to take notice of, or, worse, not notice at all. I'd rather follow a formula, answer my in-box, create the illusion of busyness and project urgency where there is none.

It's easier to measure my worth with these markers. I can point to my empty in-box as empirical evidence that I indeed did something. I have mowed the lawn, made appointments, and yes, even gone to the grocery store, all to avoid the suffering that comes with doing something different.

If you're looking for instant gratification, stay on the shores of Same. Doing weird work will often feel like rowing in the middle of a tsunami with a map drawn by a kindergartner.

One of my favorite pastimes, designed to let me avoid any kind of creative energy, has been practicing the fine art of worrying. I've spent hours on end dancing with the devil to a tune we both know by heart, the one that talks about tomorrow with the confidence of yesterday. It's a song that sings a hollow what-if devoid of any wonder or curiosity. Its melody is catchy, repetitive, and deceptively calming. Before I know it, I'm tangled in knots, convinced that safety, security, and Same are far more important than the pursuit of the Sacred Weird.

Make no mistake: weirdness is dangerous. It's uncertain. Its outcome is undefined, crude, and chaotic. Choosing to do weird work, work that comes from our deepest, truest, most unique selves, means accepting an invitation to embrace chaos and vulnerability, agreeing to use them as assets in a culture that shuns them as cancers. There is a deep connection between Same and safety, both idolizations of preservation in a culture averse to any kind of friction or uncertainty.

Allow me to get scientific here for a moment. (I'm assuming you're like me and were busy drawing flying DeLoreans during science class. If not, please excuse the following simplistic explanation.) In mechanics, kinetic friction is the force that occurs when two surfaces are moving against each other. In other words, whenever there's movement, it's often accompanied by friction.

It may just be the artist in me, but I think that timeless scientific principle spills out and pours deep into our humanity. One of the greatest hindrances to welcoming chaos and vulnerability is that we've been taught to confuse friction with fatality. In reality, friction helps create traction. It challenges the comforts around us in order to bring about an even better solution. Friction is a life giver, not a death sentence.

It's a near-foreign concept to my generation of Americans, one that grew up with antidepressants, air-conditioning, and passively segregated neighborhoods, all inventions designed to feed our constant craving for comfort and convenience. It's been hardwired into our governments, institutions, and even religious models—this plan to barricade pain and suffering out with systems, strategies, and overly simplistic storytelling.

We've been taught that fear and failure are enemies to be dispelled and medicated. We've been told to insulate ourselves from our villains and to run away from our monsters.

Why is it, though, that children create fantastic stories

about monsters lurking beneath their beds? Did they devise this idea out of thin air, or is it more likely that their parent just turned out the light, shut the door, and left the room? Could it be that their developing little minds are looking for some possible method to pull their guardian and protector out of dark obscurity and back into plain sight? It's not the monster that's scary. It's the absence of Mom or Dad. The monster is simply a narrative created to restore peace in the midst of fear. What's even more telling about this age-old tactic is that none of us have ever seen a child consulting another on this bedtime strategy before choosing to implement it. It isn't common knowledge around the sandbox that "the monster technique" works, yet it's the go-to method almost every child uses.

In response, a bad parent might keep the child in fear, threatening from the other room that the monster might pop out and eat them if they keep talking. A mediocre parent (or perhaps just a very tired one) might simply try to anesthetize the child from the other room, calling out something to the tune of "Monsters aren't real. Go back to bed."

A good parent, however, does something entirely different. They go into the child's room holding a flashlight and invite them to look under the bed, open up the closet, peer behind the curtain, and face their monsters head-on.

What Jim Henson knew when he created *Sesame Street*, what Pete Docter and the team at Pixar discovered when they dreamed up *Monsters, Inc.*, what Maurice Sendak realized when he wrote *Where the Wild Things Are*, is that we learn, grow, and flourish when we choose to befriend our monsters, when we concede the possibility that perhaps they can teach us things about ourselves if we allow them to lead us into the dark and wild unknown.

I've been attempting to bake this concept into my four-year-old's mind, recently writing her this poem:

> Don't listen much my daughter
> to the things they say of Fear
> That there are creatures in its water
> so you better not go near.
> That its citizens are giants
> who keep monsters as their pets
> Who go around devouring
> illegal safety nets.
> Yes, it's true its water is full
> of animals that play
> But the people there are much shorter
> than most outsiders say.
> So sally with your sea legs, child.
> Pray that they don't give.
> There's but a few who know
> that Fear is where the good things live.

I'm trying to remind my child (and myself) that while it may seem counterintuitive, we live life to its fullest whenever we decide we're going to dance with a monster, tango with a tarantula, polka with a piranha...you get the picture.

We've been taught to confuse friction and failure with fatality and fiasco, but the artist, the pioneer, the challenger, chooses to build her home directly in the eye of the hurricane, welcoming it as an opportunity to expose the truth and change people's minds. We flourish when we decide to move beyond what the data tells us, breathlessly wobbling on a tightrope that leads to something greater...wonder.

Wonder (n.)
1. something strange and surprising; a cause of surprise, astonishment, or admiration.
2. the emotion excited by what is strange and surprising; a feeling of surprised or puzzled interest, sometimes tinged with admiration.[xxix]

Wonder is the child of weirdness. It's the surprising inheritance we receive whenever we make a choice to plunge into the unknown, leaving Same in our wake. It's the reward weirdness gives us, a delight that results from disruption, even when things don't turn out how we might have expected. In fact, wonder makes its nest in the unexpected, the startling, and the unforeseen. When our weirdness evokes wonder, it doesn't matter what the outcome is. In the economy of wonder, even a mistake or disappointment is "tinged with admiration."

Wonder is more than mere pleasure. A zebra can experience pleasure. A rhinoceros can enjoy the sun beaming on its muddy back after a cool jungle swim. To experience wonder is to be uniquely human. There's more at stake, more to wager. It's equal parts instinctual and mathematical.

Let me explain.

Have you ever wondered why you've never seen a bear bungee jump? I have, and I think I know the answer.

You've never seen a bear bungee jump because humans are the only ones with the instinct to look at the statistics and still make a decision that might not work.

Bears don't get a rush from defying gravity. They don't acquire a sensation from disregarding the odds. In short, they are incapable of experiencing wonder.

That's not to say data isn't important. Classical musicians, for example, spend their whole lives training to play numbers and rules that have been meticulously planned out on paper. But if you give that same composition to a robot, something is lost. When a musician brings her humanity, herself to the composition, it all of a sudden comes alive and moves us.

Sometimes that musician decides that one note needs to be played a little longer, or louder, or with slightly more vibrato than the data calls for. The musician relies on her gut to lead rather than the rules in front of her... and that decision makes us appreciate the piece even more.

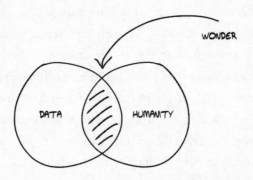

It's one thing to find your voice. It's an entirely different thing to trust it. One of the curses of living in today's digital world is our tendency to rely too much on data for answers rather than our own intuition.

But soul is what separates us as a species. Gut is what gives us our edge.

I recently heard Julie Taymor, the artist and puppeteer who brought *The Lion King* to life on stage, tell a story about the process she went through in creating it.[xxx] She recalls that although Disney executives had concerns about the contrast between her bizarre, unorthodox approach and the traditional film, their CEO, Michael Eisner, understood the strange economics of commissioning a visionary.

"Other people got scared but not…Michael Eisner. One of the first things I made was the gazelle wheel…we used bicycle wheels and the idea was to create gazelles that leap across…and I made a model of that. [I showed] the concept of not hiding the human beings…and there were some people who didn't get it who were very high up at Disney."

A few weeks later, Eisner pulled Julie aside to discuss that meeting where she'd described what was in her imagination. His response was that of a seasoned creative leader, one who is accustomed to working with weirdos, misfits, and make-believers and has learned a thing or two about how to get the most out of their supernatural abilities:

"Let's do your original concept," he said. "The bigger the risk, the bigger the payoff."

When we make decisions based on our own odd instincts, we'll find that every once in a while, we've made something more wonderful than any metric could have ever predicted.

Of course, that's not a guarantee.

Several years later, Julie went on to produce a live musical featuring the comic book hero Spider-Man. She brought the same risky unorthodoxy to her work, brought the same creative energy to the table—but it was a commercial and critical flop...a colossal one.

The reason most people never step into the destiny that their weirdness holds for them is that the risk/reward ratio Eisner spoke of isn't a hard law such as the law of gravity or physics. If Julie Taymor can create one of the most successful, longest-running theatrical productions of all time only to turn around and create an absolute flop, what hope is there for any of us?

Perhaps another way worth looking at it is, if Julie Taymor can create a flop, no one is beyond the possibility of flopping.

There has to be a deeper consideration, a more essential cause or determining factor.

Wonder.

Wonder is available and accessible to anyone willing to embrace its parent, weirdness, which we've already determined lives within every human being.

There are writers out there who will tell you to psych yourself up, believe that you're smarter and more capable of winning than you think you are.

I am not one of them.

Because you're not.

But neither is anyone.

The field is level.

And that should be wonderful news.

Julie Taymor is as capable as you are of creating something miraculous. You're also as capable as she is of creating something unsuccessful.

Unlike the bear who refuses to bungee jump, we discover wonder once we find out what to do with something that often receives a bad rap, our insecurity.

The moment we come to peace with insecurity, sink deep into the truth that every time we attempt something weird it could flop, and decide to proceed regardless, we inch closer to the type of wholeness and resilience that can only be divine.

It's God collecting Adam out of dust with the full knowledge that his creation might one day break his heart, and still calling him "very good," a preemptive description, one that can't be taken away after others have kicked it and shoved it around.

You can be both insecure and "very good" at the same time. You can create with a sense of insecurity and call what you make "very good" before it ever takes on a life of its own.

When we create from that divine place, we're accessing the Sacred Weird, the center of our soul that doesn't care what others perceive, doesn't care if what we make fits a pattern or aligns on a grid, doesn't care what the data says or what the odds are. It simply can't help but manifest what's inside, conjure it up out of ordinary dust, call it out of darkness and into light, and name it "very good."

This is why Julie Taymor continues to tinker, sketch, dream, and make long after *Spider-Man: Turn Off the Dark*. This is the deeper pool all weirdos, misfits, and make-believers keep visiting to replenish and re-create. It's the promise of wonder. It's a pull, a longing, a muscle trained to recognize insecurity and create anyway. For these people, the fear of never making anything far outweighs the fear that something might not turn out the way they imagined.

One of my favorite examples of someone who embodies this mystery is a woman named Simone Campbell, a Catholic nun known for her work alongside the poor and marginalized in the United States. "I think our sin is our obsession with security," she says. "Our obsession that everything ought to work out perfectly for us. That we ought to have every conceivable drop of oil ever that we'd ever need any time. That we have to have electricity, and…the right clothes.…I mean, all this obsession with having everything we need, security.…It's an illusion, and rather, we would be better off if we made peace with insecurity."[xxxi]

If we are going to create work that sticks out, makes a stir, or heals a divide, we must reconcile with insecurity. We must recall that our truest, most creative selves, like the ones who once named the animals and traced them in the stars, are—like the garden's first inhabitants—naked and unashamed.

Perhaps this is why Sister Simone refers to the Holy

Spirit as a mischief maker. Could it be that this mysterious Spirit comes crashing into our world like a child, with the urge to pop our bubbles and push us into the tension we so long to avoid? Could it be that she has watched every commercial ever created side by side with every tragedy and war that cycles through our human existence, and has decided that there's more to be gained from meeting each other in our tension than attempting to isolate ourselves from it unsuccessfully?

If we are going to bravely put our weird work out there into the universe, we must start becoming graduate students of insecurity, learning not only how to accept tension but how to love and lean into it.

Sister Simone has referred to this kind of dance with chaos as the spiritual act of "walking willing," a sort of contemplative, meditative practice that's concerned less with our desire for self-preservation and more with the needs that surround us: "The hard part of living the contemplative life is [what] I call deep listening: listening to the needs around me, listening to where we're being nudged and drawn, listening to people's stories, listening to the murmurs inside of me."

Usually, it seems those murmurs are an invitation to love.

To be weird is to love. To practice this strange art of surrender in a culture obsessed with winning, to give up control in a world that makes its living off selling us insurance policies. When we love, we let go when it feels much more rational to squeeze tighter. We make space in the hope that it will close a chasm. We release what we hope is a boomerang. It's completely antithetical to everything we innately believe about ourselves and others. Perhaps the weirdest thing about love is that it's almost entirely front-loaded. We feel a massive euphoric rush at first and then must trust those memories aren't entirely betraying us as the real work begins.

Like wonder, love is a by-product of making peace with insecurity. Regardless of the relationship, whether romantic or communal, when we choose love, we put our security on the line, give it over to someone or something else, and hope for something deeper and richer to manifest. Anyone who's been in a committed relationship for a long time will tell you this isn't a singular act, but rather a constant waltz with what-if.

"What if she leaves me?"
"What if they change?"
"What if we're wrong?"
"What if I fail?"

It's only when we look all the what-ifs square in the eye that our weird ideas have any shot of having power in the universe.

My friend Jeremy calls this the act of "loving anyway." A normal-looking white kid from Texas, he once had the weird idea to move to Iraq with his wife and kids to help make peace between war-torn Muslims. His organization, Preemptive Love Coalition, now works all over the Middle East crossing enemy lines, responding to crises, and providing relief to victims of war and hatred. It's a movement that started with a strange idea, one most people didn't understand. It's now grown into a global community bringing tangible hope to those who need it most.

Jeremy's relationship with insecurity is apparent. He works with people who are known for not getting along with each other, risking his life every day for them. He's been imprisoned, received death threats, and had mobs incited against him. In short, his decision to embrace vulnerability, step into chaos, and willingly choose insecurity has not always had positive outcomes.

I visited Jeremy in Iraq in the winter of 2015 to do some identity work with his team. It was there that I witnessed this insecurity firsthand. As we drove down a narrow alley at a snail's pace on the way to a team member's house, our tires kicked up dust clouds that nearly obscured the sight of a few children playing soccer. With them were two or three men in uniform, standing on both sides of the alley about three feet away from us, producing a canopy of intimidation over our passage with their large semiautomatic machine guns.

The presence of children gave me a little solace—and by a little, I mean that I was able to keep anything from making its grand Middle Eastern exit from my body for the moment.

I spoke to the driver, trying hard to smooth out the nervousness in my voice but at a pitch last heard by teachers who taught me in middle school: "I guess security is pretty tight around these parts with those police out on the street."

"Oh, those aren't police," he said. "Those are private

security guards. That house belongs to the family of a former ISIS warlord. He was killed last year."

Oh, good, I thought to myself. *I feel much better.*

When I've talked to Jeremy about all this insecurity he lives with, all the death threats, the time he's spent in prison, he downplays it, almost as if he's insulted at the idea that a few negative outcomes would possibly overshadow the massive amount of good he's encountered and cultivated—the relationships he's built, the work he's done to mend seemingly impossible divides, the family he now shares, and the lives he's seen saved. What Jeremy knows is what every weirdo with a movement eventually discovers—that the driving force behind anything that creates positive change is love.

Love is the nucleus that propels movements. It's the kinetic energy that sparks belonging. When people feel love, they feel responsibility. They feel solidarity. They feel ownership. They feel chemicals polka-dancing around their brains. It's scientific, social, and at the same time deeply personal.

When people experience love, they're compelled to make things happen.

Chapter 13

Strange Love

How sad it is that we give up on people
who are just like us.
—Fred Rogers

Shortly before my trip to Iraq to visit Jeremy and his
team, I was standing about ten feet away from a moving freight train headed toward Alabama on the coldest
January day Nashville had seen in years. I had moved to
Nashville from Southern California three months earlier,
back when the leaves were bright orange and yellow, still

glad for the hint of southern humidity that allowed them to stay connected to their owners.

Today the trees were gray and desperate, holding up their arms in austere protest to all things warm and colorful. The town I'd moved to seemed to have undergone a kind of Jekyll-and-Hyde transformation due to the abrupt absence of green and sun.

I had set up shop in a brick building that used to be a train station. My friend Pete and I were sharing office space, trading ideas and referrals and assisting with each other's projects from time to time. I met Pete on one of my many trips to Nashville before moving. Now that I was here living in town, it didn't take much time before the two of us were thick as thieves.

Pete is from the South, Kentucky to be exact. His southern drawl and easygoing personality are like comfort food to anyone who crosses his wide and welcoming path. He instantly became a big-brother figure and had a knack, I came to learn, for getting his friends to do gutsy things, persuading them, not through jabbing, bullying, or peer pressure, but with a kind of mischievous childlikeness that never quite left his face, even when he was attempting to be serious.

Perhaps that's why I warmed up to Pete so quickly. I had moved to Nashville to live a little bit more, go on some adventures, see what I was made of, and kindle the Sacred Weird within. Days earlier my prayers had been filled with these kinds of requests, supplications to the Divine to open up moments that would shake me into recognition that I was alive and it was a gift. Little did

I know that just a few months later I'd be on a plane to ISIS territory, but not before what occurred on that frigid January day.

There's this great deli just across the street from where Pete and I had our office, run by a husband and wife who put love and soul into everything they make. Around noon, Pete suggested we go get lunch. There was just one problem. In between our office and the deli were train tracks, and at the moment a three-mile-long freight train was barreling its way down them.

It would be ten to fifteen minutes before we could cross safely...and we were hungry.

Seconds after we closed the office door behind us, Pete turned his head and looked at me with a big grin on his face.

"What do you think we should do?" he asked impishly.

"I guess we'll have to wait," I said.

He paused a moment.

"You want to jump it?" he replied.

In the course of what was probably about three seconds, my entire body (brain, nerves, heart, and limbs) convened to create a narrative about why this was the greatest idea ever proposed. First of all, Pete was from the South. This was probably something people in the South did! A natural occurrence in a region FULL of trains. Second of all, I had just been thinking about how I needed some more adventure in my life. This seemed liked the perfect opportunity. Third of all, it wasn't as if the train were moving THAT fast...probably ten or fifteen miles per hour at most. If I got some speed, I bet I could grab on to the rails and maneuver through those cars pretty easily.

Three seconds later, after the bodily meeting had adjourned, I responded to Pete.

"Let's go."

A second later I was running full speed ahead toward the moving train. I jumped with all my might, and as if I had been a blues-traveling cowboy pioneer my whole life, I mounted that sucker as if it were a piece of cake.

It honestly kind of surprised me, the ease with which I grabbed hold and hoisted myself up, the fluidity with which I snaked through the cars, balancing myself between the hitch to get to the other side. I was living the southern dream. CJ the Kid was alive at last and on the loose.

I was so instantly full of myself, nothing could have made its way into my inflated ego to prevent what happened next.

I had successfully made it to the other side and was now standing at the edge of the car. All that was left was to simply jump off and land on the jagged rocks around the metal tracks. I started to feel just how cold it was outside. The distance from the train to the ground seemed a lot higher on this side than the other. With a deep breath, I plunged with confidence off the moving vehicle. Gravity and inertia did a weird dance, pulling me in all sorts of directions, but I managed to land on my feet!

Well...foot.

Very, very hard on one foot.

On the jagged rocks.

On the coldest day of the year.

I'd heard the term *cold snap* before, but now I had an acute sense of what it might mean.

I hobbled over to the sidewalk and leaned against the wall of the deli's storefront when it occurred to me that Pete was nowhere in sight.

A few minutes later, after the train had passed, I saw Pete looking at me with a bewildered smile on the other side. Apparently no one thought to bring up during my three-second bodily coalition the possibility that Pete may have been kidding.

Leaning against the wall, trying to do my best James Dean impression while in reality masking the excruciating blizzard of pain mounting around my right foot, I casually waved to Pete as he walked over.

"Wow. I didn't think you were really going to do that. You ready to go inside?"

"Yeah, well, you know me. Just living life on the edge."

I began limping toward the door.

"You OK?" Pete asked.

"Oh yeah, I think I just got the wind knocked out of me when I jumped off."

At that moment I heard a crack come from somewhere inside my ankle.

"Acccccctu-ow-ly, I think I may have sprained my ankle a little."

"Huh...well, let's get you inside then."

Once inside the deli, I recounted the completely un-necessary heroic event between bites of my sandwich and veiled winces. Pete and I both narrated the story to the deli's husband-and-wife owners, and I suggested they name a sandwich "the Train Jumper" after me. The whole time we were sitting inside at the counter, I was hoping for the pain to subside. Instead it kept getting worse. I still wasn't sure exactly what I had done to my foot, but, as a chronic idealist, I repeatedly shrugged it off and hoped for the best.

After lunch I gingerly got up, pushing my hands against the table to support myself, slowly left the counter, and made my way outside. Once back in the icy, insipid sunlight, I struggled to walk just a few steps.

"Hey, why don't you lean on my shoulder?" Pete offered.

"No, that's OK, man. I'm fine."

"You don't look fine. Lean on my shoulder."

I reluctantly obliged.

We managed to get a couple more steps in, with me wincing more with every tiny advancement.

"I've got an idea. Why don't you just hop on my back and I'll carry you back to the office?"

No. Absolutely not. That was clearly out of the question. Sure, I could imagine wounded soldiers leaning on each other after a brave and bloody Civil War battle, but show me one picture of a Union guy giving another a piggyback ride! That image just sucks any camaraderie or valor out of the situation.

"No, that's OK. We're almost back to the office."

We weren't.

I tried to walk a little farther. We were getting nowhere.

"Come on, man. Just climb on my back. I think you probably broke your foot."

I was beginning to wonder about that too, but on the off chance that I'd only strained it a little, I didn't want the rest of our friendship to be filled with stories that started off with "Hey, remember that time you were such a wuss I had to give you a piggyback ride back to the office?"

Enough was enough, though. I couldn't stand on my feet anymore. Even though Pete probably weighed only a few pounds more than me, I reluctantly climbed on his back and let him hoist me the rest of the way, hoping no one was watching this strange event unfold.

The next day I went in for an X-ray. As I was sitting on top of butcher paper like a sandwich waiting to be wrapped up, the doctor opened the door and asked, "So how did this happen again?"

"It's not really important," I replied, my cowboy ego completely bankrupt at this point. "What is it?" I asked. "A hairline fracture?

She let her glasses slip to the tip of her nose, tilted her head down, and focused her eyeballs straight at me as if to say, "Are you kidding me?"

"It's a clean break," she replied. "You're going to need surgery."

I spent the next several weeks on crutches, but I spent those first few crucial, embarrassing moments quite literally leaning on Pete. In a world that celebrates numbers and glory, Pete took one look at my strange, nonsensical act of adventure, an act that hadn't ended in pomp and circumstance, but rather in awkward, painful hobbling, and carried me through it. I'd done nothing to deserve his help, and there was nothing for him to gain but a heavy load and a sore back.

It reminds me of when Samwise Gamgee decides to carry Frodo across the toothed and snaggy mountains of Mordor when Frodo can't walk on his own any longer. There is no guarantee of success. In fact, it looks as if all is about to fail.

Yes, love is the stuff of movements, but it often looks far less cool and sexy than the silver screen suggests. Instead love often looks like people carrying each other. It walks weirdly, with a heavy load and a sore back. Oftentimes it's difficult to find those willing to engage in that version of love, who are willing to stick around with us in our weird-ness, especially when our weirdness doesn't seem to be of any apparent worth. It's truly a strange thing to "walk willing" alongside another's wild search for the child they once inhabited.

Then there are those quiet, constant people whose arms our true weird self can slip into without panic or second-guessing, whose simple presence whispers with the assurance of a battle cry, "You have nothing to prove." I have learned how rare those individuals are, diamonds among billions of grains of sand. On the surface their weirdness may seem simple, even ordinary, their kindness more interested in the load it carries than the attention it gains.

I'm done wanting fame. I'm weary of chasing wealth. Charisma has eluded me when I seemed to need it most. I just want what these scarce whisperers have. I've met fa-mous people, wealthy ones too, folks who have charmed their way to the top. None of them seem to be arrested by the kind of inescapable joy these mark leavers seem to embody.

I'm tired of living life white knuckled. I want to release my clenched fists and exchange them for open arms. I want to widen my welcome. I want to expand my capacity to love beyond what's simply convenient or constructive.

I hope my attitude and actions toward people today continue to bring them joy long after I'm gone. They don't need to be big or grand, just kind and intentional.

It's amazing that kindness is now a weird concept in our culture, a genuine way to stick out in a sea of Same. I suppose it just serves as a reminder that our weirdness is less about the attention we receive for being extraordinary and more about the gifts we're able to offer amid our ordinary life.

There's the kind of different that aims to be different only in comparison to someone else. Then there's the kind of different that comes with learning to love both ourselves and others at the same time. The former is always at the mercy of the tide rising and falling with our perceptions. The latter is wholly independent, soldered, and rooted.

I don't think we're created weird solely for our own sakes. I think we're created weird so that it's easier to love. The more we feel at home in our own skins, comfortable with our imaginations, and courageous about our capacity to create, the more we're able to leave room for those things in others.

I once heard someone describe marriage as two people

looking at each other naked, seeing all the dings and dents and spots and parts that have faded over time and saying, "I have some of those too. I still choose you. Do you still choose me?"

I've heard a lot of marriage advice from plenty of pseudosages over the years that didn't necessarily leave me in a more hopeful disposition, warnings like "Marriage is work—nothing like the honeymoon" or my favorite, the foreboding classic "Just wait until you have kids."

But this image has stayed with me for years, mainly because I think it's equal parts realistic and hopeful. It not only invites me to recognize my own oddities when considering my partner's, it shows both our oddities as pathways to deeper intimacy.

Same is a seducer. Weird isn't always sexy, but it's sustainable.

It's as if the essential reason for our weirdness is to generate belonging. That almost seems like a paradox, doesn't it? How could the act of sticking out possibly help us fit in?

I once heard a company use this as its tagline: "Be together, not the same." I really like that. Our communities aren't walls, bricks homogeneously slapped on top of one another. They're puzzles, intricate tapestries that are just as interesting to zoom in on as they are to admire as a whole.

There's a well-known phrase, "Show me your friends and I'll show you your future." While I agree with that as a foundational principle, the older I get the more I want to distance myself from the cliché. I think it's because that phrase is often used to suggest that we should fraternize only with people we want to emulate or who can help us get ahead in life. The problem is, that's not how our world gets any better.

Our world heals, expands, and comes alive when we choose instead to go to the outcasts, the misfits, and those on the margins of society, when we allow their weirdness to push up against ours, when we discover with joyous surprise that the things that connect us far outweigh those that divide.

In this scenario, we recognize that we too are the misfit. We too find ourselves on the margins of Same. Suddenly there is no "us" or "them." There is only the Sacred Weird.

It's worth saying again: weird isn't sexy. It's easy to make our weirdness all about us, as if we deserve attention, acclaim, and accolades just for being a precious and unique little snowflake. But we're not weird so other people will take notice of us. That may be a by-product, but it isn't the point. We're weird because it's the best way to show others they belong in a world that often tells them they don't.

The second you decide to use your crooked nose, your awkward smile, or your offbeat perspective rather than hide it is the second you'll find a whole bunch of people who now feel permission to be themselves too.

A few years back, I visited Tokyo for the first time. A Japanese leadership company had heard about some of the identity work I was doing with organizations and flew me out to train them on some methods I'd been experimenting with.

It's about a fifteen-hour flight from Nashville to Tokyo. I stepped off the plane in that time-drunk kind of stupor and was promptly greeted by the local consultants who had flown me out.

"We're taking you to a pool," one of them said.

Somewhat surprised the word *hotel* hadn't come up in any conversations yet, but still coasting off the last bits of adrenaline left in my bloodstream mixed with the undeniable excitement of being immersed in a brand-new culture, I replied that I was up for anything.

Now, *anything* is a funny word. Most of us use it often in a hyperbolic sense until something like the situation I'm about to describe happens.

After about forty-five minutes of driving we arrived at what appeared to be some kind of a day spa with several large wading pools filled with warm water from natural hot springs. Emi, the woman in our group, went off to visit the females-only section of the spa, while the three men, Hayato, Steve, and I, all headed to the male section.

Have you ever been in a situation where you're just along for the ride, asking yourself "What's next?" every step of the way? I live for those moments, and I quickly became aware that this was absolutely one of them.

As I passed by strange vending machines full of personal items like underwear and deodorant toward the men's locker room, I made some kind of remark about the fact that I forgot to pack a bathing suit.

"You won't need one," Hayato said.

Once in the locker room, I was given a small towel and told to strip and put my clothes in one of the lockers.

The "I'm down for anything" mentality was quickly fading as I envisioned headlines back in the United States reading "Writer Dies Naked and Humiliated at Strange Spa in Tokyo."

We exited the locker room, my very small towel wrapped around my waist, and made our way toward the main event, a gigantic room of multiple pools of varying sizes full of multiple men of varying sizes.

Every one of them completely naked.

I'm not sure if there's a Guinness World Records entry for the most naked guys in one room, but if there is, this room was definitely giving the current record holders a run for their money.

The moment I had known was imminent the whole time had finally come.

It was time to drop the towel.

With all the false bravery I could muster, I set my towel down and made the long, breezy walk toward the pool.

During this out-of-body experience it dawned on me that I was doing all this in front of two gentlemen who had specifically paid me money to consult them, spent funds to fly me all the way from another country on the other side of the world, and put me up in a hotel (which I was growing fonder of by the second at this point). Was this some kind of power play or something? Was this their way of saying, "Hey, we appreciate you coming and all, but let's get one thing straight. Just in case you think you're better than us, we're going to strip you down to nothing before we even begin"?

The three of us immersed ourselves in the steaming water. I was surprised at how instantly curative and calming it was, as if the aches and pains of a fifteen-hour journey were being individually addressed and removed.

Sitting across from me, Hayato explained that this place was called an *onsen* and the pool we were sitting in was filled with water from a natural hot spring. This was the Japanese cultural equivalent of going to the pub after work. It's where people came to de-stress, get to know each other, perhaps work out a business deal or have an intimate conversation.

I was struck by the comparison.

In the West we intoxicate ourselves in order to become vulnerable. In Japan they simply get naked.

This wasn't a power move. This was a move toward communion.

There's this communal resilience in Japan that I wish we could bring over to the West, a support for each other that transcends one's projection of one's image. There's hardly any homelessness, people buy only what they need, and family units generally stick close together.

Hayato told me that when a big-box department store tried to expand to Japan a few years ago, it failed miserably. People just couldn't comprehend the concept of buying things in bulk, especially if they are poorly made. Why not buy a few things of excellent quality instead?

We could use a little of that communal mind-set here

in the West. We could use a leveling of the pomp and circumstance that so often shrouds our true selves from connecting to one another. We might give way once in a while to the idea that the community is more important than the individual, a stretch for a society that's cut through mountains just to make a name for itself.

On the other hand, what good is a community if it's blind to the Sacred Weird among its people?

Hayato also mentioned that one of the reasons his company had brought me out was that, as communal as Japan is, that mind-set can often lead to groupthink, stagnation, and a fear of the unknown. He explained that the Japanese have a difficult time accepting those among them who might want to break free from the herd mentality and stick out with a new idea. While their culture has historically proven itself excellent at microinnovation, making drastic improvements to inventions like the automobile, it currently has very little appreciation for those who desire to follow in the footsteps of someone like Henry Ford and create "the very first" of something.

I sat there personifying the countries of Japan and the United States in my mind, wishing they could sit down together naked in a swimming pool and remind each other of what was truly important, apologize for past crimes against one another, and gift each other with the presence of a quiet, listening spirit, void of any coverings or masks.

One of the subjects we talked most about during that trip was belonging. During one of our conversations,

Hayato and his team of leaders described to me the Japanese philosophy of *ba*, a word that roughly corresponds to the English word *place*. The term refers to any kind of space that creates and shares knowledge. The space can be physical (such as a building or, say, a pool), virtual (a platform like email or video), or even mental (shared experiences, ideas, or ideals).

More transformative than normal human spaces, *ba* is a type of "place" that provides both individual and collective knowledge. It can be defined as "the recognition of the self in all"[xxxii]—the type of space that fosters meaning and a deep sense of belonging, the kind that generates understanding and insight both for an individual and for the community as a whole.

"The recognition of the self in all."

I could sit there and meditate on that phrase for hours.

Is that not the definition of love? Does that not echo the "beloved community" Martin Luther King Jr. spoke of and longed for? Is that not Christ's message of the Divine indwelling? Is it not the Sacred Weird found in each one of us?

I think the philosophy of *ba* can most easily be summed up in three simple words: *I'm with you.*

It's these kinds of spaces, the ones that evoke *I'm with you*, that weirdos, misfits, and make-believers are tasked with creating, because these spaces fit the very shapes of their souls, filling the chasm each one feels. Something as simple as a pool could create transparent belonging, an invitation to exchange knowledge without barricades or false pretense. It's a space that welcomes individuality while offering community, that promotes togetherness without uniformity.

Of the phrases we collectively came up with after our time together in Tokyo, my favorite was *Be here, bring others.*

It's one thing to be a weirdo, a misfit, a nonconformist. It's another to be a "transformist." That's what the rest of this book is about.

You're weird to show others that weirdness belongs.

There's another phrase the ancient Hebrew scriptures use, one that lives in the same family as words like *qodesh* and *nephesh*. It's *tikkun olam*. It means "repairing the world" or, better yet, "construction for eternity."[xxxiii]

It seems our souls (*nephesh*) are set apart (*qodesh*) for a grander purpose (to construct the kind of world where what's cracked is made whole).

This is the stuff of movements, the secret weirdos with a mission understand. True community and belonging are such potent and generative forces that when you unleash them, you move beyond people's need for food, shelter, or class and touch a deeper desire: the desire for love.

You're weird to illuminate to the people around you the liberating possibility that misfits matter in a world all too eager to keep things banal, to keep all the Whac-a-Moles whacked and hiding in their burrows. Your weirdness, the holy creativity inside you, finally exhaled for others to see, causes this beautiful domino effect with the power to create, share, and expand our knowledge of humankind and its place in the universe.

If you're wondering just how to go about generating this domino effect, the next chapter and the final section of this book are dedicated to giving you some examples of weirdos who have created these kinds of "I'm with you" communities, recounting their struggles, triumphs, and learnings along the way. Though some have passed from this earth, all have leaped toward their weirdness, creating, risking, and experimenting...and have lived to tell the tale. Some I've held intimate conversations with. Others I've studied and admired from afar. Some are household names. Others are busy changing the course of history in seedlike obscurity.

Let their experiences ignite your imagination. Resist the urge to compare and contrast. Simply allow their Sacred Weird to speak to yours and echo back those words,

I'm with you.

Chapter 14

Gangs, Grannies, and a Girl from 7 Mile

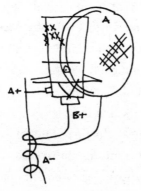

These are the days of miracle and
wonder.

—Paul Simon,
"The Boy in the Bubble"

I broke down crying in my rental car in the middle of the South Side of Chicago. For a minute I didn't really know why. And then it hit me. I had seen art. Real art. The kind of art that changes things, things like minds, hearts, systems, and cultures.

I had first heard about Theaster from a TV interview I saw him do a few months before. He was a broad, bearded African American man with a sense of peace and conviction that radiated through the television screen. I did a quick internet search for his email address and found one. My email subject line read, "I have to visit you."

Theaster Gates has master's degrees in fine arts, urban planning, religious studies, and ceramics. Simply put, he knows a few things. In addition to being an internationally sought-after installation artist, he also serves as the director of Art + Public Life at the University of Chicago. But here's the real reason I wanted to visit. While most people would be content with that vast array of titles and successes, Theaster had his eyes set on a wider canvas— a vision to completely revitalize the dilapidated, gang-entrenched South Side of Chicago...using art.

Theaster knew that in order to accomplish this mission, he'd need to make the first of many weird decisions. He'd have to reject many of the comforts that being an esteemed university professor and in-demand artist afforded him. He'd have to literally cross over the train tracks that lay just blocks away from the University of Chicago.

He'd have to move in.

Amid strange looks and scratched heads, Theaster settled into a small broken-down house on South Dorchester Avenue formerly used for a variety of illegal practices. Skilled in the art of architecture, he began transforming his new home inch by inch into what would become a work of art—a library of black culture, history, and imagination, eventually open to the public.

If that wasn't wild enough, using what he calls a "circular ecological system," he bought and rehabbed the next building on the street by selling artworks made from the scrap material from his first renovation.

Since then, Theaster and his foundation, Rebuild, have purchased and reimagined multiple houses on the same block that serve as spaces for art galleries, film viewings, child education, and personal development. There's the Archive House, which holds over fourteen thousand books. There's the Listening Room, with eight thousand records, many of which came from a local record store that was forced to close.

As I meandered in and out of each building they've purchased on South Dorchester Avenue and witnessed the collection of vintage *Ebony* magazines, the after-school tutoring that was currently in session, the backyard where a film showing was scheduled for the end of the week, it was as if someone had stuck a jet propeller to the back of my tired, cynical brain. Theaster refers to this as illuminating "the social imagination" and calls his art the art of "social practice" because it involves people and communities in collaboration, dialogue, and social interaction.[xxxiv]

I asked how he and his team have been able to influence the neighborhood so deeply. Their response was that they made a conscious decision to physically place themselves in the center of the space they sought to change, to live among the people they wanted to inspire, eliminating boundary lines, partitions, and any excuse to disconnect.

After my visit, I climbed back in my rental car and drove just three or four blocks before I found myself stopped at a red light next to a gas station. It was about noon on a weekday. The thick, gray sky full of pregnant clouds had begun to unleash its morning harvest on my windshield. Out of nowhere, just a few feet away in the gas station parking lot, sirens interrupted the peaceful tapping of raindrops as several police swarmed a man and arrested him over the hood of his car.

That's when I lost it. That's when I fully realized where I was. I wasn't standing in a museum admiring a painting. The protective casing had been shattered. The velvet ropes were lying haphazardly on the floor. This wasn't just life making art. This art was making life, the kind of art I wish I'd learned about in grade school, the Sacred Weird on display, exporting hope, cultivating belonging, and changing history for good.

* * *

On the corner of a slowly gentrifying street in east San Diego there's a studio with state-of-the-art recording equipment modestly tucked inside an old warehouse. This is where Brandon Steppe brings his weird idea to life. I met Brandon during the brief time when Kelly and I were living in the most southern part of California. Like many freelance engineers nowadays, Brandon often worked out of his garage, which he'd converted into a home studio. On hot summer afternoons, when he would open his garage door, the neighborhood kids would come by looking for their big break in the world of hip-hop. Buried just below the surface of this unwelcome intrusion, Brandon spotted an opportunity to bless his neighborhood. If a kid pulled up his or her grades he'd record a track for them. That's correct. Brandon began trading professional studio time for better grades.

This unorthodox exchange grew into what is now known as the David's Harp Foundation, a fully functioning nonprofit organization that inspires and educates all kinds of at-risk youth through music education, sound engineering, and multimedia production.

There's no magic in what Brandon is doing. He's simply opening up a passageway to a generation of capable kids whom society has sadly closed its doors on. A student may come to the David's Harp Foundation looking to be the next Jay-Z. That's all right with Brandon. He can work with it. That drive is a good beginning. His next step is to stretch his student's imagination and present him or her with the possibility that he or she is smart, worthy of an education, and capable of accomplishing the hard and often unsexy work it takes to buck the odds and realize one's vision.

For example, sometimes the opposition to a weird idea doesn't come from outside forces, it comes from within. The weirder an idea is and the more capacity it has to help others, the longer it takes for people to accept it, and the easier it is to quit.

Brandon would be the first to tell you about the times he's spent driving in his car bargaining with God, hoping he'll take the burden weirdness can often feel like away from his soul. He'll let you know about the countless hours he's spent doing things that don't feel like him at all (like fund-raising and administration) just to do what feels so much like him he can't help it.

One day at a time, one foot in front of the other, Brandon continues to embody the spirit of that ode: "We are the music makers and we are the dreamers of dreams." He continues to show up. He continues to alter the trajectory of a generation one kid at a time. He continues to place himself at the center of chaos, moving his boat out into the crashing waves while the placid beaches of California's coastline move farther away from view.

I want that kind of restless devotion. I want a fistfight with the Divine to see my weird ideas through, that roller-coaster sinking feeling in my gut that constantly asks, "Are we really doing this?" I want to drown in the waves of unexpected adventure, only to be resuscitated by the reality that any art worthy of ushering into this world is an art that risks, fights, and loves. I wish someone had told me that in elementary school. Instead they taught me how to use safety scissors.

* * *

Sugata knew kids were smarter than most of us were giving them credit for, especially the ones furthest from our mental radar, kids who live in the poor, rural, disadvantaged corners of the globe we all share. An educational researcher and professor of technology at Newcastle University, Sugata Mitra is chronically curious. He's spent his life testing weird solutions to complex problems when it comes to education all over the world.

For example, several years ago he began traveling to remote villages in India, conducting an experiment he called "the hole in the wall." He'd pick a public square where children would gather, carve out an opening in some wall, and stick a computer inside it (thus creating an excellent example of the virtual and physical *ba* we talked about in the previous chapter). What he discovered fascinated him. Children who'd had no prior access to computers began not only learning to use them with ease, but teaching other children how to use them as well! He repeated his experiment over and over again in different regions, getting the same results each time.

Sugata didn't stop there, though. He kept pushing to discover ways these kids could learn more, faster in order to compete with students in the toughest schools around the world.

While continuing to conduct more tests, he made an important discovery: simply having someone present with these children while they were learning, someone to say "Wow! That's amazing! How did you do that?" increased their scores by 20 percent. Saying wow, it seemed, carried immense transformational power, power that could be transmitted by nearly anyone from anywhere, as long as they were paying attention.

That's when Sugata came up with his weirdest, wildest idea yet. That's how the Granny Cloud was born.

I came back to England looking for British grand-mothers. I put out notices in papers saying, if you are a British grandmother, if you have broadband

and a web camera, can you give me one hour of your time per week for free? I got two hundred in the first two weeks. I know more British grandmothers than anyone in the universe. They're called the Granny Cloud. The Granny Cloud sits on the internet. If there's a child in trouble, we beam a gran. She goes on over Skype and she sorts things out. I've seen them do it from a village called Diggles in northwestern England, deep inside a village in Tamil Nadu, India, six thousand miles away.[xxxv]

Outrageous ideas, when explored and tested, have the power to solve outrageous problems. As my priest Becca says, "Insight is preparation plus surprise." What I love most about Sugata is his unabashed, mischievous willingness to be surprised.

Surprise is the pre-grown-up version of caffeine, sometimes keeping a child up all night on birthdays and Christmas Eves. It's engine fluid, helium, food for wonder. Often when I pray, it's that God will "give us this day our wonder bread."

But surprise often feels unwanted once we're introduced to Same. How many times have we kept our weird ideas from legitimately helping others because we were unwilling to be surprised by the results? How often have we predicted the outcome, sentencing an idea to death, before ever mustering up the courage to conduct our initial experiment? Imagine Sugata had convinced himself that his conjectures were too silly, his hypotheses too far-fetched, and his asks of strangers too bold. Imagine he had never placed a computer in the middle of a remote village, or pressed "send" on his Craigslist ad, for fear that his curiosity would come up empty.

Instead Sugata is inching our global community forward, proving that weird ideas like Skyping grannies and hole-in-the-wall computers can stretch across historical chasms and create the future we imagine, one where geography doesn't determine a child's opportunities to learn, create, and teach others.

* * *

After the 2008 recession, the once-booming city of Detroit became little more than a ghost town. People left the city in droves. Those who did stay just tried to survive. Jobs were scarce, and consequently so was any form of culture. Somewhere amid this regression, Samantha White grew up in the neighborhood of 7 Mile, a street characterized by violent crimes and gang affiliations. Samantha, however, kept her mind occupied elsewhere. A self-described drama geek, Sam fell in love with Shakespeare and his works during middle school after her mom caught her listening to Salt-N-Pepa and made her read *Hamlet* instead.

"You like lyrics?" she said, tossing an old hardcover book on her bed. "Read these."

What began as a punishment became a passion. Perhaps that was her mother's plan all along.

After a brief time traveling and discovering what the rest of the country had to offer, Sam made a decision many who leave Detroit never do. She returned home. She came back to the city she was born in, the city she had always loved. It was during this homecoming that a weird idea began to electrify the restless energy inside her. She would start a Shakespeare company as a way to help revive her weary town, a place that had forgotten how vital the arts are to a city's endurance.

"We wanted to create a template where we perform [where] people live, work, and play," she told me. "If we were just doing theater in theaters, it would be much more difficult for us to get people to actually show up to those shows. Instead we're going to the places they're going to be anyway. They're going to recycle their stuff, so we might as well pop up with a play and give them some Shakespeare.

"I am so grateful, shocked, and just giddy that this has even happened. We've engaged with three thousand people in less than eighteen months, and the fact that that's happened is really remarkable for a girl from 7 Mile. There's nothing extraordinary about me except that I just don't give up."xxxvi

Samantha also opened up to me about how difficult an undertaking bringing her weird idea to life has been for her and those who have journeyed with her. Fund-raisers have gone south. Neighbors have struggled to understand her motivation as she went door-to-door inviting them to free shows being held in recycling centers and city parks.

But there was one performance in particular that keeps the Sacred Weird alive in her. It's a production of *Romeo and Juliet* she directed at her high school alma mater, a school with an auditorium that had never been used for a play.

Just stop and think about that for a moment. A high school auditorium with a stage, lights, sound equipment, and seats had never once been used for a play.

Until now.

A few hundred people huddled to watch her team's raw and riveting performance, many of them high school students who had never heard of Shakespeare before, let alone seen a theatrical production.

You could hear a pin drop.

After the show the cast and crew came out to do a question-and-answer session with their mesmerized audience. When the play's director took the stage, the students were shocked to see Samantha, a young African American woman, standing in front of them—a woman who'd attended the same school they did just a few years earlier.

This was a play in itself, a story more remarkable than the one they had just seen. There, standing on that stage, was proof to these students that another narrative is possible for them and their city, a different one than they grew up hearing, a proclamation of hope that Detroit in fact isn't doomed, that a bright future is indeed possible, and, most importantly, that someone exactly like them could birth part of it into being. Perhaps they're not the problem. Perhaps they're the solution.

Samantha explained this possibility to me in her own words.

If along the way some other kid from 7 Mile, or 6 Mile, or 8 Mile [where Eminem grew up]...if they see me, they can be like, "Maybe we can do it too." Because the thing is, for me growing up, I didn't think it was possible for me to do anything. I had a vivid imagination, but when we would turn on the news as kids (national and local), all you would hear is "Detroit is awful. It's violent. The people are bad. Everything about Detroit is bad. If you go there, there's nothing but awful buildings."

So if you're a kid from Detroit and everything you hear from people is about how awful Detroit is, you start to think you're awful. "Hey, I'm from that awful city so I must be awful too." So for me, if a kid from Detroit hears another awful Detroit story, they'll remember me and go, "You know what? That's really not true. If Sam did it, I can do it too. I can be whatever I want to be."[xxxvii]

In other words, weirdness begets weirdness. There's a communal awakening that happens when someone carves a different path from the one those stuck in Same are used to. When weird ideas start working, they carry with them the remarkable ability to bring along others, creating movement. It may not look like a massive rush of people at first, but that's OK. Movements should never be confused with flash mobs.

Flash mobs are exciting, surprising, and, yes, at times even weird, but flash mobs by their very nature are only fair-weather friends, here today and gone tomorrow, much more forgettable than movements, which are more concerned with the long game, the sustainable, the culture bending, and the kind of influence that divides.

If the beloved narratives of our culture are any road map, once a misfit decides to move, a pattern almost always follows: other misfits begin to come out of the woodwork and help!

For every Batman there's a Robin.

For every Luke Skywalker a Han and Chewie. For every Frodo a Samwise, Legolas, and Aragorn.

And yes, for every Rudolph there are those who find themselves trapped on the Island of Misfit Toys (feel free to imagine me rolling my eyes as I type right now, because that's exactly what I'm doing).

The point is, there's something generative about sticking out by sticking up for others, by championing belonging and togetherness in a world where those qualities are in short supply. It doesn't matter if they're gang members from the South Side, kids who think they're the world's next big hip-hop stars, grannies with a webcam, or a scrappy group of thespians from 7 Mile. When weird ideas work, they're not only restorative, they're reproductive!

Weird ideas, and those courageous enough to materialize them, not only revive the imaginations of our communities and move them closer to wholeness, they remind us that true togetherness transpires from awakening our shared uniqueness, the wild what-if each one of us carries, not just for ourselves, but for the fellow weirdos traveling in our midst.

Together, that's how misfits start movements.

Part 3

How Your Weirdness Will Change Us

Chapter 15

Misfits Start Movements

Here's to the crazy ones. The misfits.
The rebels. The troublemakers. The
round pegs in the square holes. The
ones who see things differently.
They're not fond of rules, and they
have no respect for the status quo.
You can quote them, disagree with
them, glorify or vilify them. About
the only thing you can't do is ignore
them. Because they change things.
They push the human race forward.

—Apple commercial, 1997

I grew up in the nineties, which meant that if you were lucky enough to have cable, on almost any given weekend you could find *The NeverEnding Story* playing on TV. It's a fantastically campy movie filled with flying dogs, boulder people, and a synthy soundtrack that's out of this world. The main character is a shy, creative boy named Bastian with an affinity for reading old books. Within the first fifteen minutes of the film we find out that he's recently lost his mother. Because of this tragedy, his relationship with his father has become strained. If that isn't enough, he's got a gang of school bullies after him who call him names like "weirdo" and routinely throw him in the dumpster.

When Bastian stumbles upon a strange book called *The NeverEnding Story*, he discovers that the world is on a collision course with destruction and nothingness.

"People have begun to lose their hopes and forget their dreams," he reads. "So the Nothing grows stronger.... It's the emptiness that's left. It's the despair destroying the world."

Eventually Bastian realizes that he has the power to rescue the world from the Nothing. First, though, he must put his faith in what seems utterly ridiculous to him throughout the film: the idea that a loser, a reject, a misfit like him can make a difference. Only when Bastian decides to start dreaming again, to trust that his weird imagination holds the power to change things for the better, does the world begin to move away from the Nothing and back toward hope and harmony.

I love that movie. It reminds me that misfits, weirdos,

and make-believers, whether Jesus Christ, Harriet Tubman, Albert Einstein, or Susan B. Anthony, not only have the power to start movements, they're usually the only ones who can.

Like Bastian, I remember being picked on when I was a kid, mostly about my being shorter than the other kids, as if for some reason my inability to reach a book on the top shelf made me less of a human or something.

No one wants to be small.

Napoléon hated it too, so he went around starting wars and conquering countries and naming ice cream combinations after himself. It's amazing what our desire to do something tremendous will drive us to.

Everyone wants to be a movement.

Just what makes a movement a movement, though? After all, that's a word that seems to get thrown around with increasing flippancy these days. Simply adding the word *movement* to a cause, campaign, or communications strategy doesn't automatically make it one.

If you're like me, you've heard this word used to a nauseating extent over the past few years by coffee brands, magazines, retail chains, speakers, preachers, and everyone in between. Our culture has become obsessed with "big." The language we use to lure people to whatever we're selling is overly seasoned with descriptors like *catalytic*, *relevant*, *revolutionary*, and *exponential*. It's not enough to attract people anymore; our number one goal is to get people to join our movement.

Twentieth-century American writer Eric Hoffer wrote, "A movement is pioneered by men of words, materialized by fanatics, and consolidated by men of action."[xxxviii] Later, however, he went on to say that "every great cause begins as a movement, becomes a business, and eventually degenerates into a racket."[xxxix]

On its surface a movement is about generating something gigantic. But as we've discussed, sincere movements, the sustainable, truly influential kind, are more concerned with division than with multiplication. While the word *movement* might have us all fixated on doing something seismic, there's more to the word than we're giving it credit for. Consider its definition in the context of a musical composition.

In music a movement is a small, unique part of a much larger whole, one of multiple sections and story lines that make up an entire composition. Each movement carries its own tempo, cadence, or rhythm that repeats itself throughout, beautifully and cyclically reminding listeners of its particular imprint and expression in relation to the big picture.

True, abiding movements are interested in creating unique rhythmic patterns that speak to a much larger whole. Rather than degenerating into a racket, they build upon each other, creating a symphony.

Movements are unmistakable, strange, and wildly effective forces that are hard to stop once they've picked up steam. They rarely happen overnight, and they never happen by accident. If we are to heed Hoffer's warning, we must recognize that there is a heavy weight to the word *movement*, a responsibility that accompanies its energy. In order for a movement to stay a movement, it must keep its long journey toward change the priority over the lure of short-term sustainability. In other words, if movements are to avoid becoming irrelevant, they must fight to keep themselves *irreverent*.

Movements are, in essence, weird.

A truly sustainable movement gathers people around something meaningful in order to create change. Every movement begins with an invitation to embrace something different, a unique point of view that stands in direct defiance of Same. This gives movements the advantage of a distinct identity. On the other hand, it also makes them extremely vulnerable. Before movements are remembered for being extraordinary, they're questioned for being weird.

You can take any movement and filter it through that two-part narrative: Christianity, democracy, women's suffrage, surrealism, rock and roll, the civil rights movement, punk, Disney, Apple, etc. Before any of them changed the culture, they were met with varying amounts of skepticism and concern. Each one of them was a Whac-a-Mole well acquainted with the snozzberry effect.

So what does this mean for you and your weirdness? How will your Sacred Weird change us for the better? How will you move your team, your classroom, your family, your audience, or your community toward the future you imagine?

Throughout history, you can track virtually every oddball with a movement on the following journey of translating their mission to those who need to hear it:

1. Find the Weird: Every movement has something completely unique about it that makes it stand

out in a sea of Same. But it's not until it discovers and defines exactly what that is that things begin to snowball.

2. Gather the Weirdos: When a movement owns what makes it weird, a crazy thing happens—others start to join in. These like-minded people who become partners, patrons, and participants are often fellow misfits just waiting for someone else to say, "I'm with you."

3. Make the Manifesto: Next it's time to share the weird with the world. The greatest movements accomplish this through manifestos. These movements learn how to take their weirdness and translate it in a way that makes sense to others.

4. Hack the Culture: Finally movements hit a stride when they're able to make believers out of those who initially overlooked them. This tough act of changing minds and permeating culture is accomplished only after the first steps.

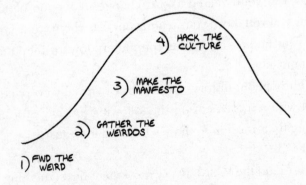

I don't care if you're a Founding Father, a freedom fighter, Jesus Christ, or a PTA member, your new and different idea needs to run through this process in order to make the conversion from obscure to orthodox.

In the next few chapters, let's unpack each of these four phases one by one.

Chapter 16

Fred Got Fired: How Weird Ideas Become Movements

If you're loved by someone you're never
rejected.
Decide what to be and go be it.
—The Avett Brothers, "Head Full of
Doubt/Road Full of Promise"

Fred was in his early twenties when he first turned on a
television set. It was the late 1940s and the medium
was just picking up steam. His parents had just bought the
cube-like state-of-the-art device and placed it in their

living room in accord with many other middle-class American families.

Fred had grown up, by many accounts, a weird kid.

He was quiet and shy, with an atypically empathetic disposition for someone his age. He had just finished college and was about to enroll in a seminary to become a minister, but what Fred saw when he turned on that set sent a shock wave of indignant conviction through his young, lanky body.

Pies being thrown at people's faces. People hitting other people and abusing them. Slapping. Punching. Demeaning. Sure, it might have all been in the name of comedy, but there had to be a better way to use this influential medium that was so rapidly becoming the very centerpiece of the American household.[xl]

Fred knew what he was imagining was different, maybe even weird, but it didn't matter. Shortly after this virgin viewing experience, he decided he himself would pursue a career in television. Several years later a different type of program beamed into living room TV sets. It was a weird program, full of puppets and trolleys and brightly colored cardigans. Armed with those strange props and a simple but profound message, *Mister Rogers' Neighborhood* revolutionized television forever and became one of the most successful children's programs of all time.

More fascinating and less known is that the beloved series was briefly canceled in 1967 due to a lack of funding.

That's right. Mister Rogers got the ax.

But something happened: a small but vocal public demanded he be put back on the air.[xli] They wrote letters, made phone calls, went door-to-door collecting funds, and organized. The movement Fred had begun wouldn't be stopped so easily. In 1967 the Sears Roebuck Foundation picked up the bill to fund future episodes of *Mister Rogers' Neighborhood*, a decision that allowed the program to be seen in more households across the nation.[xlii]

A few years later, after President Nixon proposed budget cuts to public television, the quiet, lanky neighbor sojourned to Washington, D.C., to testify in front of the US Senate Subcommittee on Communications and make a passionate case for public television and shows like his. Sitting in front of Senator John O. Pastore, the chairman of this particular subcommittee, he waded into a respectful but determined defense.

"This is what I give. I give an expression of care every day to each child, to help him realize that he is unique. I end the program by saying, 'You've made this day a special day, by just your being you. I like you just the way you are.'"

Rogers, a master of show-and-tell, didn't just stop there, though.

"Could I tell you the words of one of the songs, which I feel is very important?" he inquired.

He then launched into one of his numbers from the show, "What Do You Do with the Mad That You Feel?"

Pastore, who was known around Washington for being an ornery character, had apparently never seen Rogers's show. By the time he was done, the chairman was visibly moved.

"I'm supposed to be a pretty tough guy," he replied.

"And this is the first time I've had goose bumps for the last two days.... Looks like you just earned the twenty million dollars."[xliii]

As a kid, I remember bringing my bowl of Frosted Flakes into the living room in the mornings and tuning into the old man in the bright cardigan, trying to restrain myself from fixating so much on the world he was inviting me into that I didn't keep a close eye on my Frosted Flake–to-milk ratio, lest I incur unwanted sogginess.

My favorite part of each episode was when the trolley would whistle its way into Mister Rogers's living room. It meant a new adventure was on the way, an escape from the normal, a window into imagination and make-believe.

As I got older, though, and watched my younger siblings do the Mister Rogers Frosted Flakes–and-milk juggling act (they were amateurs compared to my former glory), I began to question some of Mister Rogers's practices, particularly when it came to the trolley. For instance, watch any episode and you'll notice his arm reaching down slightly out of the shot to press a button that obviously triggers the trolley's arrival.

I remember thinking that if I ever had the chance to meet Mister Rogers, I would tell him, "Fred, you're obviously quite successful. Don't you think it's about time to hire an intern or someone to press the trolley button for you? Or maybe a wireless remote control that you hid up your sleeve?"

But lately I think I get it.

Mister Rogers didn't need help making the trolley move. Mister Rogers knew exactly what he was doing. He knew that kids were so tuned in to his unwavering love and care for their imaginations, their futures, and their neighborhoods that he didn't need to rely on any extra machines or gadgets for help. He had mastered the art of human connection.

His brand of loving your neighbor as yourself, remembering you're unique even if you don't feel that you are, and imagining the possibilities of a world without hate was as transparent as his low-budget living room set. He lived what he preached from that living room, and he treated each of his viewers like they were the only person in it.

He knew what made him weird and owned it, religiously, without excuse or apology. Everything else, everything unimportant to his point of view, faded into the background. It was all Same to him.

Today we possess the most advanced vehicles ever invented, the latest and greatest remote controls to move the trolley. But without that human connection, that one-of-a-kind fingerprint to press the button and steer our imaginations forward, we will have settled for a culture run by robots.

Mister Rogers knew this early on, and it guided him ever after, in the wake of every storm, through the good times and the bad.

When you latch on to what makes you weird, whether you're Fred Rogers, who changed the purpose of television, Martin Luther King Jr., who radicalized nonviolence, Walt Disney, who turned cartoons into an adult art form, or the pioneers of rock and roll—when you discover exactly what makes the way you see the world wonderful, different, and extraordinary, it gives you the courage to embrace it and the clarity to communicate why it matters.

More often than not, your weirdness manifests itself as a response to a problem worth solving. Take rock and roll, for instance, a genre that originated from a literal emphasis on the offbeat. At the beginning of the 1950s, a few musicians started looking to pare down the mammoth orchestral swing bands that had characterized the 1940s. These outfits were becoming costly and unsustainable, so musicians began forming smaller groups creating wilder, more vibey sounds, textures featuring wailing saxophones, driving guitars, and accentuated boogie rhythms.[xliv]

Oftentimes, what starts as a breakdown eventually sounds like a movement.

Movements are sometimes like snowballs. Sometimes when things are going downhill, they're actually getting stronger, picking up momentum.

Like the neighbor who blessed our TV sets with low-budget simplicity infused with connective wonder, the one who continues to do so long after his body has left the earth, your movement, the meaning your weirdness brings to the world, carries with it a soul that can travel on for miles without ever tiring. Once identified and defined, it is a force to be reckoned with, one with a magnetic ability to pull others along with it.

But once you identify it, please don't doubt it. Stay in the game. Keep your eyes open. Stand your ground.

We need you to.

I need you to.

I need to be reminded that the words I've written in this book are true, that they mean something, that they aren't fairy tales but real-life possibilities you and I can step into. I've seen some plunge in and live to tell the tale, but I'd be lying if I didn't admit to the growing sadness that follows me around as I realize how many others have tapped out at the first sign of rain.

There are leaders all around us who truly desire to be different, to swim against the tide, to cultivate the future they long for, whatever that may be, but who have become all too easily sedated by Same's lullaby.

We've become men and women of anemic conviction. We've nursed a brittle backbone that breaks at the slightest hint of the insecurity and instability that might accompany our weird, potentially remarkable ideas. We've been imbued with the truth, the Sacred Weird, the reality that rests in our deepest, truest selves, and yet we question its power or relevance in the company of anyone or anything that seems like a safer bet. We are nowhere near the voice of Fred Rogers, who believed so ardently in the imaginary world he created that he put his reputation on the line, looked his threat square in the eye, and defended its place in an ordinary universe.

An obsession with Same kills a movement dead in its tracks.

I almost forgot why I was writing this book. A few hurried weeks and unplanned distractions disconnected me from the conviction that had overwhelmed me and made me begin punching out some thoughts on the subject of weirdness in the first place.

Then recently I heard the story of a minister at a church in North Carolina who was considering whether to ask a woman who had been attending his congregation to serve. This woman was a savvy leader, a brilliant creative talent, and a caring counselor. She was a woman of color, which would have been helpful to the church's leadership team, who desperately needed some diverse representation. In short, she was a remarkable asset to any leadership community.

But that wasn't enough.

She had tattoos.

Worse, she often wore short-sleeved shirts to show them off.

This plot twist created a considerable issue for the minister. It's not that he cared about her markings. He didn't believe there was anything wrong with having tattoos. But what would his congregation think? What would the conservative, Christian community that gave donations weekly believe about the direction in which the church was headed?

Are you catching the deeper enigma here?

This wasn't an old minister. This wasn't a small church on the verge of extinction. This was a young, thriving, "relevant" institution in the heart of an affluent suburb, the kind most people on the outside would consider hip, current, not your grandfather's church.

It wasn't his conviction that sent him into a what-if panic that eventually resulted in his congregation missing out on a remarkable human being, but his lack thereof.

I wouldn't be surprised if the shape of his soul looks a lot edgier and more "tatted up" than the decisions he makes. But he let Same lead the dance and allowed fear to squeeze that shape until all the oxygen had nowhere to go but out.

Fear often looks like short breaths.

This is why I've written this book. For him…and for her…though I honestly can't tell you who needs to hear this message more.

For her, I want to shake her by the shoulders and yell, "Keep going! This isn't your fault! Please, don't let someone else stop you from gifting us with your Sacred Weird. We need to keeping hearing from you and learning from you. We need you to keep rolling up your sleeves, meeting us on the shores of Same, and showing us the shape of your soul."

For him, I want to send him to the mountains somewhere far away from humanity. I want him to shut out the voices. I want him to get quiet and still enough to get weird again. I want him to let divine wonder whisper what's true apart from the emails and billboards and conversations veiled in competition and comparison that plague our daily goings-on. I want him to understand what the birds and bugs know, that their provision is the field and their sanctuary the sky.

For both of them (and all of us), I'll close this chapter with a prayer I wrote in honor of our dear, beloved Saint Fred on the fiftieth anniversary of his first show. May its verses rise to meet you and fall gently on your soul.

Help us to love our neighbor,
To see the sacred specialness in them
The way we long for others to see it in us.
Give us this day an imagination,
A place in our soul where we can make and believe
Untethered to kingdoms that have lost their will to
    wonder.
Lead us to our inner child, a place where we belong
In tennis shoes scuffed by curiosity
Where a sureness quietly blossoms in not knowing
    everything.
And deliver us from the things that hide us
That kidnap this gift, the good feeling it is
to know we're alive.

Chapter 17

Jim, Jesus, and Harriet Tubman: How Movements Gather Misfits

Yeah, well, I've got a dream too, but
it's about singing and dancing and
making people happy. That's the kind
of dream that gets better the more
people you share it with.

—Kermit the Frog

Nobody at any of the television networks understood what James was trying to do. He already had a successful kids' show on television, but James wanted to make a new kind of show, one that grown-ups and kids could watch together and equally enjoy. Unfortunately for James, after years of trying, it was clear no one was biting.

James was really good at two things, though: not giving up, and getting like-minded people on board with his crazy ideas.

It probably won't surprise you, but James Maury Henson, better known as Jim, was excellent at gathering weirdos, misfits, and wildly imaginative people from all over the world to help bring his wacky ideas to life. He'd travel the globe searching for fellow make-believers, inviting them to come work for him. It's how he met a serious teenager named Frank Oz, the voice of Fozzie, Miss Piggy, and Cookie Monster. It's how he found his longtime writing partner and collaborator Jerry Juhl. It's how he came across a struggling cartoonist turned puppeteer, Caroll Spinney, who would eventually go on to play Big Bird.

His introduction to Caroll is particularly fascinating. Caroll, who had been turned down as a cartoonist by Disney just a few years earlier, decided to act on his love for puppetry, entering puppet festivals and experimenting with new acts and ideas. During one particular festival performance, Jim happened to be in the audience. A few minutes in and the lights—a key ingredient for making the performance successful—suddenly stopped working. Caroll abruptly left the stage, frustrated and humiliated.

A few minutes later, Jim came backstage to meet Caroll. He had heard of Jim, who was already well-known in the puppetry community, but the two had never met before.

"I get what you were trying to do," Jim told Caroll in his trademark quiet, even voice. He then offered him a job on a new program he was developing with the Children's Television Workshop, an experiment they were calling *Sesame Street.*[xlv]

Jim was a master at seeing potential where others saw failure. He was brilliant at sniffing out value in people when they could barely see it in themselves. He was referred to as having "a whim of steel," a deep contrast to the kind of anemic conviction we've previously discussed. If he imagined something, he was going to make it happen, and you were going to help. Period.

In fact, do you know how Jim finally got his adult-friendly program, *The Muppet Show*, made in the midseventies? He went to England! A land full of weirdos and misfits, iconic template breakers like David Bowie, Led Zeppelin, and the Clash!

British broadcasting company Associated Television was the only network on the planet weird enough to take a chance on *The Muppet Show* after every American station flat-out refused it. Shortly after, *The Muppet Show* went on to become the single most-watched television program of its time. Not just in Britain. Not just in America. But around the world.[xlvi]

When a movement finds its weird and starts owning it, a crazy thing happens: people start to join in. They're usually fellow misfits—like-minded outsiders with similar convictions, passions, and story lines, who are often just waiting for someone else to say, "I'm with you."

C. S. Lewis once said, "Friendship...is born at the

moment when one man says to another 'What! You too? I thought that no one but myself...'"[xlvii]

Movements are me-too machines.

This process of initiating "Me too," "I'm with you," "We're together in our weirdness" carries with it an unbelievable power to reconcile. It's a mending power, a bringing-together magnetic force that takes people out of their isolation and into legitimate belonging.

This is Harriet Tubman and her network of underground railroaders, a woman who is said never to have lost one of her three thousand escapees, which gained her the nickname Moses, a woman who refused anesthesia for surgery, opting to bite a bullet instead, and the first woman in America to lead a combat assault.[xlviii]

It's the dropouts, embezzlers, and prostitutes who made up the apostles and the early disciples who gathered around Christ's strange message of radical grace.

It's the misfit fans and journalists who supported punk during its formative years inside small underground clubs teeming with teenage angst and frustration.

Movements are magnets that pull misfits toward them, people who are hungry to help and eager to belong to something that welcomes their weird dispositions. The challenge all weird ideas face is making that magnet powerful enough to pull all the right people together from wherever they are. Many call this an awareness problem, but what all movements face at some point is an attraction problem. That is, the problem of creating enough polar power to link individual outsiders around the universe, transforming them into insiders.

The French idea man Olinde Rodrigues was quite the weirdo in the 1800s. Today Rodrigues's job description would read something like "Part banker, part unrecognized mathematician, part social reformer."[xlix] To say the man was prolific would be an understatement. His ideas had ideas, some good, some pretty out there. One of his most interesting ones, however, was a mathematical premise he called *transformative groups*, which basically provided evidence that things working together rather than alone achieve greater action.[1]

Think about that for a moment. Things working together rather than alone achieve greater action.

Movements can't survive in a vacuum. They are absolutely dependent on community. This becomes a paradox for movement makers. On the one hand, we feel at home in our calling to be weird, different, and abnormal. On the other hand, we need to recognize that there's a oneness to our humanity, a pull toward genuine belonging, a connection to others we can't deny or ignore if we're ever going to grow.

It's vulnerable to ask for help. For me, it's something that's gotten harder the more I practice it. The voice of shame inside my head pipes up with persuasive punch lines like "You should know this by now" and "What will people think?"

But asking for help is not an admission of failure. It's an admission of humanity.

There's something in our tension-averse culture that breeds this idea that a need for help is synonymous with failure. Don't believe me? What do you think of when you think of the phrase *marriage counseling*?

Trouble.

Jeopardy.

Infidelity.

Divorce.

Breakdown.

Those are some of the words that immediately came to mind for me. Why? Because I grew up in a culture that said marriage counseling was for struggling marriages, not healthy ones.

But why would any partnership not take advantage of a guide willing to walk alongside it even when things *aren't* on the brink of disaster? Isn't it possible that doing so might prevent disaster in the first place?

We are wired for support as much as we are wired for solitude. When we choose to dive into what makes us different and create from that place, it can get very lonely very fast. Part of our ongoing challenge is to separate ourselves from our work, make an active effort to seek out community, and practice asking for help the way one would exercise a muscle. No one can accomplish these tasks for you. People may even turn you down when you try.

Most people are busy. Most people are unaware. Most people have their own litany of personal problems they're currently in the middle of working through.

I've put an awful lot of pressure on some people, holding them highly accountable in my heart for not responding to a message or phone call. I've created entire narratives about why they didn't have the time to engage my precious email or answer the phone, when in reality it may have just been a busy week—or worse, the inconceivable idea that my crisis is not the most important issue on someone's plate at the moment!

It's important to give those people the same measure of grace we hope for when we're brave enough to be honest with our own journeys. Remember, we're all just a bunch of grown-up kids who once got the weird kicked out of them. We all long for community, but many of us are still just dipping our toe back into the sandbox.

Don't let that stop you from spilling your Sacred Weird once you find it, from letting it overflow and stick to others. Your movement's shelf life is entirely dependent on the people you choose to share it with, especially the parts that aren't perfect. In fact, it's those imperfections, the things that aren't going right yet, that have the most power to cultivate belonging.

Sometimes it's what's *not* working that sparks the change necessary for something to grow. Not what is.

So often our organizations and communities are obsessed with finding the "right fit" when in actuality we might benefit more from searching for the "mis-fit," someone who can help shake us out of our cycle of Same and illuminate a possibility we didn't even know was there.

I'm by no means saying this method is easier or less of an investment. Quite the contrary. Weirdos, misfits, and make-believers rarely like to be contained or controlled. They're brash and zealous (think of Simon Peter, the hotheaded punk Christ said he'd use to build his church, or Frank Oz, Jim Henson's creative partner, who was known for his temper and intensity). They don't love rules and often speak truth before most people are prepared to hear it. But the inescapable reality is that the curating of rejects, rebels, chaos creators, and margin huggers has historically been the method of choice for any movement that's made a difference.

Movement happens far more often on the margins than it does in the masses. If you're wondering how to solve some of our culture's most deeply rooted problems, does it not begin there?

Could it be that we are meant simply to practice opening ourselves up to hearing "I'm with you" from unexpected voices, the voices of people we may think are nothing like us, wouldn't understand, and couldn't possibly offer us any help? Could it be that the future health of our communities, companies, schools, and governments is the acknowledgment that we are all a little weird and that's the point?

What if we pressed into each other's weirdness rather than trying to avoid it, silo it, or gentrify it?

We might find our knowledge, resources, and opportunities expand beyond what we previously thought imaginable. We might find that not only does *I'm with you* create more shared joy, it's good for business. We might find we're no longer stuck in Same.

We might find movement.

Before any of that happens, though, we need you to do something, something courageous. We need you to speak up.

Chapter 18

Walter's Memo: How Misfits Make Believers

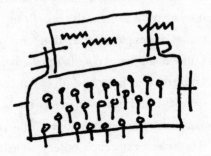

To hold a pen is to be at war.

—Voltaire

It was two days before Christmas in 1935, and Walter was tired. Tired of working. Tired of trying to convince the bank that his first full-length movie could be profitable. Tired of looking at his team's work and feeling disappointed.

He sat down at his typewriter and began punching out a letter to Don Graham, which has to be the most 1930s name one could possibly have. In my imagination Don Graham doesn't have any pigment to him whatsoever, he's just black and white from head to toe, softly lit, with a cigar hanging out of his mouth at all times.

Walter started his letter by asking Don, who was a respected art teacher at the Chouinard Art Institute (now CalArts) to train some new animators and improve his old ones.

But Walter Elias Disney wasn't just typing a letter, he was crafting what would eventually become a manifesto. It was pages full of instruction and methodology, covering details like character expression, signature style, story construction, and audience values. In short, it was a detailed blueprint of everything Disney considered important to realizing his movement's vision.[li]

I imagine him waking up the next morning, passing out copies to his animators between deep and deliberate puffs of cigarette smoke, reminding them, "We're doing something weird here, fellas. And here's exactly how we're going to do it."

What's remarkable about this manifesto is the timing of it all. His plucky team of animators hadn't yet pulled off their most audacious achievement, the first fully hand-drawn feature of all time, *Snow White and the Seven Dwarfs*. In fact, they were only midway through production. And it wasn't going great.

This manifesto wasn't an accident or an afterthought. This was purposeful, calculated, a meticulous attempt to communicate the what, the why, and the how that continues to make his work so special.

If you read his letter to Don, it's obvious that Disney is still figuring it all out as he writes, going off of hunches and instincts. He's trying to get the weird ideas in his head out and into the hearts and minds of those who need to understand them best, his motley crew of "I'm with you" weirdos, a few animators crazy enough to work for a young, scrappy artistprenuer with visions of creating eighty minutes of sequential hand-drawn film (again, something that had never been accomplished before).

We've all been where Walt was. We've all felt the Sacred Weird running through our veins with profound internal clarity and suddenly jumbling up into a chaotic hair ball of complexities and non sequiturs the very second it reaches our mouth. We've all gotten paralyzed by the challenge every misfit inevitably faces: translating their weird ideas into something that makes the slightest sense to others.

But once a movement finds what makes it weird and begins to gather others around it, it must eventually begin to put its strange point of view out into the atmosphere if it is to have any hope of convincing or convicting culture. Historically, the way movements have accomplished this (Walt Disney's included) is through manifestos, declarations, and stories, words and themes that strike a chord with those they hope to reach and influence.

Christ offered parables and proverbs. The Founding Fathers handwrote the Declaration of Independence. Before that they went around handing out *The Federalist Papers*. Martin Luther King Jr. wrote "Letter from Birmingham Jail" and spoke out: "I have a dream." Steve

Jobs launched his groundbreaking Apple ad "The Crazy Ones."

Rock and roll expert DK Peneny notes, "A musical genre does not simply appear, it gradually evolves at a point in time when some event, performance, publication, or recording allows listeners to perceive its unique qualities."[lii]

Weird ideas must manifest themselves before they can ever move people.

They've got to go through what I think looks an awful lot like that frightening tunnel in *Willy Wonka & the Chocolate Factory*. They need to travel around the corridors of your imagination's dark side, past the annex of anxiety and through the walls of what-if, before exiting naked into the atmosphere, where others can see them.

It doesn't matter what your movement is. A manifesto takes unique ideas and pollinates them for the common good. While having a manifesto is a must for a business or nonprofit, it's a great idea for a family too. Better yet, imagine the benefits creating a manifesto for a neighborhood, a classroom, or an entire school could produce.

But sadly, manifestos rarely happen, rarely ever see the light of day, because manifestos often look like lines in the sand. A leader once told me there's a difference between a vision and a reaction. It's one thing to create a reaction to what isn't working, it's another to show us what's possible. Manifestos do both. These creeds are the very definition of avant-garde in that they're radical and unorthodox, a departure from the status quo. Making them is dangerous, sobering, and consequential work.

Truth that moves us is often written with trembling hands.

Manifestos are powerful, clear, and invitational declarations. They're not mission statements that simply look nice when placed in a fancy frame or engraved on an employee's Christmas gift. Manifestos leap off the page and cause action. The words are often just the beginning.

They're the memo Jerry Maguire photocopies and sticks in his coworkers' mailboxes (before email forwards exist), the one that gets him fired before he starts his own company. They're Patch Adams's impassioned speech defending the Gesundheit! Institute to a board of crusty old doctors attempting to take away his medical license.[*] They're Martin Luther nailing the ninety-five theses to the church door, knowing very well he'll be excommunicated. They're me writing a book about weirdness, all the while wondering if people aren't ready to love the things that make them strange. It's you knowing every word to the hymn that plays in the cathedrals of your heart, unsure what it will sound like if sung out in a quivering voice.

It bears repeating: manifestos are dangerous. Putting your weird point of view out there, birthing it into the vast, dark, cold atmosphere, is, to put it lightly, some incredibly vulnerable stuff.

Let's not forget there are more than a few famous manifestos out there I'm willing to bet you don't care to agree too much with. Because they're made by humans,

---

[*]   I am referring to Robin Williams's fictional portrayal in the film *Patch Adams*. In real life, Hunter "Patch" Adams is an incredible weirdo who's spent decades helping people all over the world through the Gesundheit! Institute. You should look it up!

manifestos can be used to create good or prolong evil. Creating one forces you to take a hard look at what you'll stand for and what you won't—what kind of culture you wish to create for others and what you're willing to let go of in order to see that culture realized.

People rally around manifestos for the long run because they strike a chord with who they are at their deepest, truest, weirdest selves. They evoke the movement that's already stirring inside them and invite them to cheer, "I'm with you."

Like Walt, misfits with a movement must learn how to take their weirdness and translate it in a way that resonates with others, a way they can easily comprehend, identify with, and latch on to, becoming believers in a world of skeptics.

That's, of course, much easier said than done. Weird by its very definition "suggests the supernatural." It's difficult to explain, hard to contextualize, and even tougher to simplify. But if weird is to win in a sea of Same, movements must learn how to become artists, journalists, and publishers, transcribing the difference they make for those who need to understand it.

Because once people understand your weirdness, once their imaginations are captured, it has the power to transform them.

And changed people ultimately change culture.

Chapter 19

Weirdos and Cool Kids: How Make-Believers Touch the Masses

If the good Lord intended us to walk,
he never would've invented roller skates.
—Willy Wonka

Somewhere on Long Island, New York, during the early 1980s, my father was busy making the second-best decision of his life: he had enrolled in a night class for computer programming. At about twenty-eight years old, he had recently married my mom and was thinking about having yours truly (in case you were wondering what was his first-best decision).

My dad was one of those kids you see in a Norman Rockwell painting. He grew up in one of those classic three-story tenement apartments in Brooklyn, playing stickball in the street, going to Mass every day (performed entirely in Latin) and sneaking his way into games at Yankee Stadium to see Mantle and Pepitone spin their magic with wood and leather, hoping their powers would somehow reach him from beyond the bleachers. His environment was one of brick walls and marble altars and couch cushions carefully protected by plastic coverings. He had lost his old man, a US Army corporal in World War II, to lung cancer when he was only sixteen. At that time he also started taking art class in high school. I remember rummaging through some of his old sketchbooks and paintings in our basement as a kid, amazed even then that someone so young could be that good. At eighteen he applied for art school but wasn't accepted, something that baffles me to this day, as if being an artist is something you can get into versus something you already are.

After high school he got his associate degree at a local college and played drums in a rock and roll band, the late-seventies kind with the double stacked keyboard, one keyboard for the bass line and the other for the melody— because why split beer money among four people when you can just as easily split it among three?

They'd go from bar to bar performing Billy Joel covers with an occasional "Here's one we wrote ourselves" that only garnered more requests for "Piano Man."

By day he worked at a print shop, a job that got him

close to artwork but one concerned more with replicating than with creating.

Then computers came onto the scene.

He and my mom had been married about a year or two. After work my dad began auditing night classes to learn how to program. I imagine his ink-stained hands draped over a keyboard as he tried to decipher a language still being refined by its natives. It was worth it, though. He was finally creating again—sketching, painting, experimenting, playing—the days of cover songs and reprints rapidly vanishing behind him.

When he decided to bring up his newfound interest in computers to my mom's father, the response was less than supportive. "That's a fad. It'll never last," my grandfather said.

Needless to say, my grandfather was not known to possess vision.

He was the kind of man who gravitated toward the future like sap running down a maple tree. His shirts, pants, and opinions were all equally pressed, creased as if no amount of play could wrinkle their exact, uncompromising lines. I don't recall my young eye ever seeing him in anything less formal than a three-piece suit. My aunts tell stories of him mowing the lawn in those suits. I'm not sure what the vest was ever for except maybe to hold his pocket watch. That was how he liked to keep time— hidden, protected, preserved, wearing only its chain for others to notice.

It's probably also worth mentioning that my grand-father once tour-managed some of those big bands of the forties that preceded the rock-and-roll revolution. He even handled some little unknown opener whom he eventually fired after the young performer requested a small raise.

His name was Frank Sinatra.

Vision my grandfather had not.

Put yourself in my dad's shoes for a minute. Imagine losing your father at a young age, then marrying someone and having their dad, the only father figure in your life, tell you all the extra work you're doing, all the discomfort and inconvenience you're voluntarily putting yourself through in order to provide a better life for your family, a choice you made while navigating a life void of any role models or guidance...is a fad.

Still, my dad took to programming as naturally as he had to art in high school and soon began teaching the same classes he'd entered as a student. Nearly four decades later he's made a fantastic career developing and managing complex programs and systems as he's witnessed computers go from large enough to fill up entire rooms to small enough to fit in the palm of his hand.

What was weird to one generation, after enough misfits gathered together and created a language that translated into progress, eventually became the norm on a global scale.

Let's look at another weird shift. I've already mentioned how much I love vinyl. The early 2000s saw a renaissance of people buying records and record players. The uptick started specifically in 2007 and 2008, during the time of the housing market crisis and resulting economic recession.[liii]

I've often wondered if there is some correlation between that uptick and the state of our collective souls
during that period. At a moment in history when it felt as
if things had gotten too complicated, become too phony,
and progressed beyond anything tangible, a time when
behind-the-scenes operations failed us without punishment, an era when the concept of "the cloud" was just
being introduced to the mainstream culture, a point when
people were losing everything, present and future hopes
swiftly dissolving from their grasp, could it be that humans were simply looking for a representation of simpler
times, an experience they could hold in their hands, a nos-
talgic kind of quality they could sense and trust?

I may be overthinking it. The parallel is fascinating,
though. Regardless of what catalyzed it, the vinyl resur-
gence is one of the most interesting movements of the
early twenty-first century. In the digitally dominated age
of the MP3, what started out as a weird idea (let's go back
to listening to music on vinyl) that gathered weirdos (music nerds, audio junkies, and collectors) and had a creed
(because it sounds better while offering a more holistic experience) eventually broke its way into the mainstream.

Today, you'd be hard-pressed (I'll wait a moment to let
that brilliant dad joke sink in) *not* to find a record player
for sale in any conventional, run-of-the-mill department
store selling its brand of "cool" to the masses. Modern
recording artists are even choosing to print their records
on vinyl and getting top dollar for them.

Why would something so inconvenient and archaic
find its way into the mainstream? Why would retail stores

built around the very concept of modern convenience start selling such an extraneous piece of technology?

How did a musical movement that once sat peacefully on the fringe trickle its way into the masses? The same way rock and roll, punk, and hip-hop did. They hacked the culture.

This phenomenon isn't limited to wax and needles. Any movement, from the most surface fashion statement to the most complex ideology, always begins with weirdos and eventually seeps into the rest of culture. It doesn't matter if it's a start-up, communication medium, ideology, or social enterprise. What the cool kids once made fun of they've now adopted as their own. From skinny jeans, nerd culture, bottled water, laptops, and online dating to larger paradigms like racial inclusion, religious freedom, space travel, and globalism, what was once seen as radical is now normalized.

While weirdos ought to celebrate the moment they discovered what makes them weird (like Fred Rogers), gathered like-minded believers (like Jim Henson), and created a manifesto (like Walt Disney), the next and hardest feat lies in transforming those who don't quite get it yet.

Weird ideas hit a new stride when they're able to speak to their skeptics, converting those who may initially overlook them for a variety of reasons such as fear, unawareness, ignorance, or indifference. Throughout history we've seen this happen to every major movement from Christianity and democracy to civil rights and personal computing. In the twenty-first century alone, movements like podcasts, coworking, electric cars, online education, and minimalism quickly come to mind. The process of hacking the culture (or, as I like to call it, "the normal-sphere") is the methodical practice of gathering enough weirdos to spread the same cohesive message to the masses that it eventually ceases to be weird.

Breaking into the normalsphere may seem like victory, and in many ways it is. But it should never be viewed as a finish line. In many ways it is just the beginning. This method of finding the weird, gathering the weirdos, making the manifesto, and hacking the culture is better looked at as a cycle, not a linear plot with a definitive end point. Instead, hacking the culture simply becomes a turning point. It poses a new challenge for weirdos who have triumphantly drilled their way into the normalsphere with a concept that once seemed foreign and strange. As Eric Hoffer warned a few chapters back, "Every great cause begins as a movement, becomes a business, and eventually degenerates into a racket."

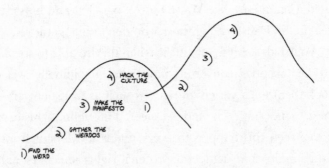

Once weird becomes normal, movements become clinical, ubiquitous, and stagnant. When stagnation sets in, irrelevance inevitably follows. In order to keep growing, a movement must begin to find what's weird again. That's most obviously true for a nonprofit organization, enterprise, or political office, but it's equally true for a friendship, marriage, or family. Regardless of what context we find ourselves in, if we bank on things to constantly stay the same we'll be disappointed at one of two inevitable outcomes: either they will and we'll find ourselves bored, ineffectual, and distant, or they won't and we'll be confused, disappointed, and unprepared.

Weirdness is a muscle that needs to be flexed. After a movement has successfully hacked into the very culture that once doubted it, it's left with the often scary task of taking a step back, looking inward, and reimagining what's possible. For weirdos to keep their movement sustainable they must always find the courage to roll up their sleeves, erase the whiteboard, and go back to the beginning, away from the turning tides and trends that clamor for our attention.

There's one trend happening in pop culture right now, I wonder if you've noticed. It seems everything is being named a "collective." There are artist collectives, design collectives, restaurants called collectives, businesses that bear the name, and so on.

While the importance of collecting people should not be undermined, what the future will need, however, is *re*collectives.

Ancient mystics refer to recollection as the practice

of withdrawing one's mind from all things external and earthly in order to focus on the Divine. For a movement to sustain itself into the future it must perform this ancient art of recollection, a stepping away from all things Same to reconnect with the Sacred Weird.

This process happens only in silence and solitude. It's said to only be achieved by "the avoidance of distracting and dissipating occupations not dictated by reason or required by necessity."[liv]

That's a tall order for most of us who find ourselves trapped in a hyperconnected, sense-stimulating society. To say that it's counterintuitive would be an understatement. How many moments throughout our days are filled with ancillary tasks or occupations that fail to meet the criterion of being "dictated by reason or required by necessity?"

Sometimes I think it would be a good idea to become Amish-ish. Not full-fledged Amish. I love an electronic device every now and then, but I wouldn't mind adopting just a few of their principles for the sake of creativity, centering, and occasional solace. Cherry-picking, if you will. (Do Amish people pick cherries? I don't know, and as an Amish-ish person, I search for things on the internet only when absolutely necessary.)

In fact, in the same way an Amish teenager experiences *Rumspringa*, I think I might encourage my kids to become Amish for a year to experience a full season's worth of solitude and simplicity, free of distractions or external voices that scream that what they have isn't enough.

At some point every last one of us needs to get low. Get quiet. Get undistracted…before we can ever get weird again.

It's one thing to be a nonconformist, another to be a transformist, and it's an entirely different thing to repeat the process all over again.

But the act of recollecting ourselves often gives us the power to generate something new, something different, something that wakes up our imagination again.

Several years ago, a few musicians made an unexpected discovery. They decided to record the sound of crickets chirping. When they played the recording back at a much slower speed, they heard what appeared to be the soft, steady sound of monks chanting in unison, a calm, deliberate chorus complete with reverent, meditative undertones.

I didn't believe it, so I had to listen myself. My arthropodan exploration led me through a labyrinth of message boards, audio recordings, and amateur video clips. It turns out this miraculous phenomenon is real!

These small, abundant pasture dwellers, when relaxed, compose a choir of supernatural proportions. Why is it, I wonder, that the life of a cricket is so surprisingly short? If they only knew they didn't have to move so fast in order to bless the earth, didn't have to grind their gears at such a breakneck speed to give us their strange gift, perhaps they would live longer than only two or three months at most.

It seems to me the willful ritual of slowing down and becoming quiet, the act of listening more deeply than we're taught or used to, carries with it the strange ability to turn noise into music.

Recollection always leads to a renaissance.

What exactly was it that triggered Da Vinci to sketch the first flying machine or motivated Michelangelo to tear down ceilings stroke by stroke and reconstruct them into heavenly windows? To begin, the Hundred Years' War had finally ended, ushering in an era of peace and tranquility. The Black Plague, which killed an entire third of Europe's population, had at last subsided, causing those left to reflect on what was important when sudden death was no longer a threat. In addition, sacred texts began to emerge from monasteries thanks to the invention of the printing press. For the first time in history, people were visiting libraries and attending schools to reconnect with the Divine through ideas and scriptures long forgotten and ignored by those in search of power and self-preservation.

History's most prolific creative era materialized out of one defined by scarcity, solemnity, and soul-searching. If you're going to catch lightning in a bottle, you'll have to transcend the storm. Recollection reminds us that if we are going to ever create anything beautiful, lasting, and worthwhile, it's going to come from who we are when we are stripped of all our striving.

I was sitting down with a friend of mine who's a song-writer. He began sharing with me the process he recently went through in making his last album. He had an idea to travel the country for several months, visiting cabins, farms, and retreat centers, quiet havens of solitude, with plans to write a song at each stop. He packed up his guitar and a few small pieces of recording equipment, filled up his tank, and began his voyage just as the sun was rising over the east Nashville hills.

A few hours later he nestled into his first cabin off the coast of North Carolina. Three full days went by, and not a word was written. He took long walks, picked at his guitar for hours, stared at virgin sheets of notebook paper, and sat in vigilant silence. Still nothing. Over the next several weeks, he traveled to his other marked spots, remaining faithful and disciplined to the same routine in each. At the end of his trip he came up completely empty.

He returned home discouraged, deeming the entire trip a failure. The next day he locked himself up in his studio and, as if a spigot had suddenly and violently loosened, the entire album came to him in a little less than a week.

The trip itself wasn't the prolific tsunami of inspiration he was expecting. Before he left, his life had grown increasingly chaotic and noisy, his psyche strained by challenges and changes all playing off each other in double time. It turned out he needed to recollect before he could experience a renaissance, something every make-believing misfit needs to make a sustainable difference.

At some point our families, our communities, our teams, our schools, our lives…all need a renaissance, a brave awakening of our weary imaginations.

Christ called it the process of being "born again," going back to the beginning, when we didn't know everything and didn't dare think we could.

It's a humbling, stumbling kind of posture, a deliberate choice to approach the world like a child, adopting fresh ears that wistfully, almost frantically listen for the call to adventure, arms that fearlessly stretch to catch the next branch in hopes it will take them where their imagination leads.

As children we spend magnificent amounts of time

constructing blanket forts, drawing maps, and deciphering kingdoms out of cloud formations. No one needs to tell us to do this or how to go about these procedures. The instinctive urge to create worlds that have never existed before, to literally see what's unseen and speak it into reality without fear or shame, is an urge we possess incredibly early in our development as human beings. By the time we find ourselves sitting in a cubicle, however, that natural, often daily practice has been reduced to an occasional far-off gaze unenthusiastically accompanied by phrases like *if only*.

This is because at some point in our adolescence we were told to abandon our blanket forts, throw away our maps, and assimilate to the way the world really works. At some point we got the weird kicked out of us. Maybe it was a teacher. Maybe it was a bully. Maybe it was a parent, a boss, or a coach. For most of us it was a combination of all these people, some well meaning, others ignorant, all of them damaging.

Over time we were conditioned to believe that the kind of nonsensical thinking we were used to as children had a nonnegotiable shelf life, and that shelf life was over.

The message we should have heard as children (the one we hopefully tell ours) is that our innate ability to imagine is one of our greatest human assets, a talent so incredibly valuable that it should never peak at the creation of a blanket fort. It should never settle for stagnation. Instead it should mature with us as we get older, the same way a four-year-old learns how to count to ten but a fourth grader progresses to long division.

I'm convinced this is why we need to keep the glue

of our humanity, our organizations, governments, schools, communities, all the way down to our closest, most intimate relationships, alive and percolating with imagination. We must always be searching for weird! We must always be cultivating the astonishing, the fantastic, and the avant-garde.

It's time for a renaissance. It's time for a rebirth. It's time to go back to the beginning.

We must continue to fight for the child inside us all before the weird went away, the child who greets the darkness and asks, "What might you be hiding?"

And make no mistake: it is a fight. But it's one that makes you remember why God created that child in the first place, why you're still standing on the cliff of an ever-expanding atmosphere, your heart beating in rhythm with a cosmic symphony for some strange, imaginative purpose buried there from the very beginning.

Your weirdness has the capacity to change us and help us belong. Earlier, I reminisced about *The NeverEnding Story*, but I never mentioned the best part . . . the ending.

In the last few moments of *The NeverEnding Story*, all that is left of the world of imagination is one tiny grain of sand held in the palm of the Childlike Empress who rules it. Everything else has been taken over by the Nothing.

Only when Bastian decides to keep dreaming and imagining can the land be populated once again.

Bastian and the empress stand amid a sea of complete darkness.

"Why is it so dark?" asks Bastian.

"In the beginning it's always dark."

Chapter 20

Go Down the Slides

Who is the happy Warrior? Who
is he
What every man in arms should wish
to be?
—It is the generous Spirit, who,
when brought
Among the tasks of real life, hath
wrought
Upon the plan that pleased his
childish thought:

Whose high endeavours are an
inward light
That makes the path before him
always bright.
—William Wordsworth

In the beginning we were weird. And in the end we'll go back to the beginning.

As children, we instinctively followed our sacred imaginations, before their light was snuffed out by the normalsphere. When all is said and done, when the world finally heals, when we become who we're meant to be, it will be because we learned to go back to where we started.

The ancient mystics long pontificated on the concept of the good life, a life that transcends suffering, a life available to those in touch with their true selves as well as their fellow man's. A life so powerful, so sustainable, that it keeps giving and regenerating forever and ever, a perpetual renaissance that triumphs over resistance. The Taoists refer to it as the Way. The Buddhists call it nirvana. I think I like Christ's name for it the best, the Kingdom.

This is undoubtedly in part due to the fact that, like my daughter, I grew up unable to avoid the intoxicating indoctrination of all things Disney. I was like a seven-year-old hospital patient hooked to a constant IV drip of talking animals and "I wish" songs. I can vividly remember my young, financially struggling parents patiently filling a giant water cooler bottle of pocket change over the course of about two years to pay for our first trip to the Magic Kingdom. I can recall looking at the jug filled to the brim with pennies and nickels and hearing my mom confirm, "It's time."

That's how strong the Disney brand is. I've got a heartfelt story locked deep inside my brain, one that planted itself long before I was able to make my own decisions. And it's not even a commercial! It's real life!

Now, as a parent, I understand Disney's cyclical effect. It's not only marketing to my daughter on her diapers; it's still marketing to me! It knows that most days I'm far removed from the boy that once leaped and galloped through adventureland, concerned far too much with more important matters like tomorrow's deadline, the mortgage, and how the sod seems to be coming in. It knows the only thing better than going back and reliving the Magic Kingdom as a kid again would be to live it vicariously through the wide-eyed excitement of my daughter.

Those clever, sneaky, brilliant geniuses.

In the gospels Christ is always talking about a magic kingdom to grown-ups preoccupied with getting things right. He hands out free admission to a weird upside-down world where the poor are rich, the last are first, and the lost are found. And the greatest news is that it's here, on earth, just as it is in heaven! To Christ this wasn't a mere fantasyland. It wasn't some enterprise to be commoditized, marketed, or exploited. You could enter it immediately, if you chose to see it with the eyes of a child. He was Willy Wonka announcing that the snozzberries taste like snozzberries! To which the proud and ignorant replied, "Who's ever heard of a snozzberry?"

Throughout this book you've learned not only why you're so weird, but what to make of it, and—even more thrillingly—how your weirdness can change us for the better. Hopefully, the common thread you see stretching from page to page is this: the person you're capable of becoming has a lot to do with the kid you were taught to forget.

Why is the force of Disney so infectious to children?

Why does Wonka hand the keys to his factory to a ten-year-old?

Why does Christ use the silly to confound the sensible?

Amid a shallow sea of Same, perhaps there's something deeper at play.

It's because when we're young, the Sacred Weird runs around fully alive in our playful rambunctious selves before Same comes lurking around to steal, kill, and destroy it. When we're children, we're predisposed to believe in the fantastical, the imaginative, the bizarre, and the impossible. We're walking resurrected souls, innocent and liberated. We are smarter than our adult selves, closer to the Divine who, like us, sees architecture in our scribbles and masterpieces in our messes.

I'm trying to go back there. I've been hitchhiking across picture books and chasing after windmills. I've been trying to find creatures in cloud formations, something I used to do so effortlessly but now rely on my daughter to guide me through. I've been looking at my neighbors and the people I pass by, trying to uncover the fantastic beings in them as if they were those grade-school folders with the optical illusions printed on them.

It's so hard. I've gone blind. We all eventually do. The Same, the Nothing, fills our lungs with soot and tar even after the smoke settles.

But I want to see the world through Kingdom goggles. I want in on that good life where misfits like me matter. I want to look at my surroundings, beginning with my soul, through the lens of the Sacred Weird, through the wild what-if wonder of my childhood, the kind that jumped first and dreamed often.

I want that for you too. I want you to know that whatever made you weird as a kid, whatever captured your imagination before it was stolen away by pirates, has the remarkable and holy capacity to help people belong today, beginning with your own self. I want you to access the Sacred Weird, the wild what-if that's buried alive deep down in your soul. I want you to risk stepping off familiar shores to discover you might just find yourself with the strange ability to walk on water.

There's a remarkable phenomenon that happens every day, all over the world, on playgrounds in every city. If you pay attention, you'll notice it. It happens on the slides.

The next time you visit a playground, watch what happens right before a kid goes down the slide. They all do a version of the same thing. They all make the same instinctual gesture.

They look.

They look to see if someone is watching them, someone who loves them, someone who cares for them, someone who will acknowledge that they're proud of them.

There's a deep, fundamental need in a child to be seen whenever they're about to take a risk, especially by someone who cares about their well-being.

If no one has ever told you this, it's my honor to be the first.

You are loved.

You are seen.

Now go down the slides.

The Weirdo's Manifesto

Imagine a world where we all loved what made us different instead of succumbing to a constant barrage of comparison and conformity. There would be less anxiety, less bullying, less war, and a whole lot more joy. Our art would be better. Our businesses would stand out. Our kids would know they're loved just the way they are. Imagine a world where weird wins.

It already does; many people just don't know it yet.

Sadly, most of us grow up believing it's more important to fit in than to stand out. After a while, shame, comparison, and conformity creep in until we forget all about this strange and incredibly powerful thing inside us, an imagination, that can change things around us for the better.

But there's something different about each and every one of us...and it matters. What if our weirdness was the key to changing everything? What if the outrageous, imaginative, crazy ideas that live inside our wildest dreams are actually there on purpose to help others belong in a world that often convinces us otherwise?

Embracing our weirdness is the best thing we can do for our art, our business, our friends, our family, and ourselves. It's the essence of creativity, the stuff of movements, and the hope for humanity.

It's time we took back what makes us different, and reimagined the difference we were born to make. It's time we quit following the rules, conforming to patterns, and checking off boxes. It's time we stopped settling for "Same" and reclaimed the word *weird*.

Weird is awesome. Weird is remarkable. Weird is transformative. It's rock and roll, Jesus Christ, Mister Rogers, and Martin Luther King Jr.

Weird is a revolution.

Our weirdness is contagious and viral, and it comes preinstalled. When we bravely decide to embrace the Sacred Weird within us, it lets others know they belong too, causing a ripple effect with the power to create and even transcend culture.

Don't get swallowed up in a shallow sea of Same. Don't settle for a paint-by-numbers existence.

Be outrageous. Choose different. Get weird.

Acknowledgments

To Kelly: Thank you for loving misfits, this one most of all. Your fearlessness wakes me up every day. From the front porch to the backyard and everywhere in between, here's to being uniquely matched.

To Bill: Thank you for teaching me what love looks like. Your fingerprints are all over this book.

To Roy: Yours too. Thanks for seeing a version of me I wasn't brave enough to yet.

To Mom: You didn't just teach me to color outside the lines, you taught me to draw my own. For that I'm forever grateful.

To Dad: Thank you for watching me go down the slides.

To Sarah: You're a poet and a priest. Your love for words can be outweighed only by the way you command them. Thanks for letting me sneak a few of yours into this book.

To Aaron: Thank you for talking me off the ledge more than once. With every passing year, I'm exponentially more grateful for the rarity that is our friendship.

To Lynn: One day you'll know just how many seeds you've planted.

To my friends in Japan: I'm grateful no ocean is great enough to prevent dreams from sailing to each other.

To Monty: Thank you for suggesting the supernatural.

To Whitney and Esther: Thank you for believing in this weirdo.

To Virginia: Same goes for you. Sorry for all the commas.

To you who bought this book: That's a big deal. You have no idea how big a deal it is. In a world where you can spend your money on anything—anything at all—I'm honored you chose to spend it on these words. I hope they've served you well.

Endnotes

i *Random House Unabridged Dictionary*, based on the Random House Unabridged Dictionary, © Random House, Inc. (2018). Definition of "weird." http://www.dictionary.com/browse/weird?s=t

ii Genesis 3:9–11 MSG

iii 1 Corinthians 1:27

iv https://www.greatsemioticians.com/en/algirdas-julien-greimas

v Matthew 11:17

vi Flannery O'Connor (1988). *Collected Works: Wise Blood / A Good Man is Hard to Find / The Violent Bear it Away / Everything that Rises Must Converge / Essays and Letters*, volume compilation, notes, and chronology. Literary Classics of the United States, Inc., New York, NY. All rights reserved.

vii https://www.ted.com/talks/ken_robinson_says_schools_kill_creativity

viii "Modern Living: Ozmosis in Central Park," *Time*, October 4, 1976 (online archive of *Time* magazine). The quotation appears as an epigraph at the beginning of the article.

ix Gwen Moran, "These Will Be the Top Jobs in 2025 (And the Skills You'll Need to Get Them)," *Fast Company*, March 31, 2016. Retrieved from www.fastcompany.com/3058422/these-will-be-the-top-jobs-in-2025-and-the-skills-youll-need-to-get-them

x Stacey Boyd, "Extracurriculars Are Central to Learning," *U.S. News & World Report*, April 28, 2014. Retrieved from www.usnews.com/opinion/articles/2014/04/28/music-art-and-language-programs-in-schools-have-long-lasting-benefits

xi Valerie Strauss, "The Surprising Thing Google Learned about Its Employees—And What It Means for Today's Students," *Washington Post*, December 20, 2017. Retrieved from www.washingtonpost.com/news/answer-sheet/wp/2017/12/20/the-surprising-thing-google-learned-about-its-employees-and-what-it-means-for-todays-students/?utm_term=.e3c6a84f2a1c

xii Thomas Merton (1955). *No Man Is an Island*. The Abbey of Our

Lady of Gethsemani, copyright renewed in 1983 by The Trustees of Merton Legacy Trust.

xiii   Romans 8:1–2 MSG

xiv   Romans 12:2, MSG

xv   Matthew 6:12-15 ESV

xvi   http://www.taoistic.com/taoteching-laotzu/taoteching-79.htm

xvii   https://www.bustle.com/articles/117928-10-things-that-were-considered-weird-in-1995-but-are-totally-normal-now-according-to-reddit

xviii   Frederick Buechner (1973, 1993). *Wishful Thinking: A Seeker's ABC.* All rights reserved. Harper Collins Publishers.

xix   https://researchblog.duke.edu/2016/02/03/bigger-church-less-engaged-parishioners/

xx   joakimsunden.com/2013/04/the-agile-coach-role-at-spotify/

xxi   https://www.biography.com/people/james-lawson

xxii   https://www.tennessean.com/videos/news/local/2017/02/20/rev.-james-lawson-his-1960-expulsion-vanderbilt/98173782/

xxiii   Sinéad Burke on *The Moth* (podcast), March 15, 2016. Transcript at https://themoth.org/stories/break-a-leg

xxiv   Thomas Merton (1961). *New Seeds of Contemplation.* The Abbey of Gethsemani, Inc., published in arrangement with New Directions Publishing Corporation, 80 Eighth Avenue, New York, NY, 10011.

xxv   C. S. Lewis (2001). *Mere Christianity: A Revised and Amplified Edition, with a New Introduction, of the Three Books* Broadcast Talks, Christian Behaviour, *and* Beyond Personality. HarperSanFrancisco.

xxvi   John O'Donohue on *On Being* (podcast), August 6, 2015. Transcript at https://onbeing.org/programs/john-odonohue-the-inner-landscape-of-beauty/

xxvii   Matthew 18:1–5

xxviii   Nassim Nicholas Taleb (2012). *Antifragile: Things That Gain from Disorder.* Random House.

xxix   *Random House Unabridged Dictionary,* Based on the Random House Unabridged Dictionary, © Random House, Inc. (2018). Definition of "wonder." http://www.dictionary.com/browse/wonder?s=t

xxx   http://www.wnyc.org/story/htt-julie-taymor/

xxxi   Simone Campbell on *On Being* (podcast), June 10, 2015. Transcript at https://onbeing.org/programs/simone-campbell-how-to-be-spiritually-bold/

xxxii   Ikukiro Nonaka and Noboru Konno, "The Concept of 'Ba': Building a Foundation for Knowledge Creation," *California Management Review*: vol. 40, no. 3, Spring 1998. http://home.business.utah.edu/actme/7410/Nonaka%201998.pdf

xxxiii   http://www.nscblog.com/miscellaneous/what-is-your-tikkun-olam/

xxxiv   http://www.tate.org.uk/context-comment/articles/who-is-theaster-gates

xxxv   https://www.ted.com/talks/sugata_mitra_build_a_school_in_the_cloud/transcript#t-1014048

xxxvi   Excerpt from *The Sounds Like A Movement Podcast* by CJ Casciotta.

xxxvii   Excerpt from *The Sounds Like A Movement Podcast* by CJ Casciotta.

xxxviii Eric Hoffer (1951). *The True Believer: Thoughts on the Nature of Mass Movements.* Harper and Row, New York.

xxxix   Eric Hoffer (1967). *The Temper of Our Time, Essays.* Harper & Row, New York.

xl   Tom Junod, "Can You Say...Hero?" *Esquire,* November 1998. Retrieved from https://www.esquire.com/entertainment/tv/a27134/can-you-say-hero-esq1198/

xli   *"Who is Mister Rogers (1968)?" Independent Star News* (Pasadena, California), April 28, 1968. Retrieved from https://clickamericana.com/eras/1960s/who-is-mister-rogers-1968

xlii   http://thefw.com/10-things-you-didnt-know-about-mister-rogers/

xliii   http://www.huffingtonpost.com/entry/mr-rogers-pbs-budget-cuts_us_58ca8d6fe4b0be71dcf1d440

xliv   Robert Palmer (1992). "Church of the Sonic Guitar." *Present Tense.* Duke University Press.

xlv   *I Am Big Bird: The Caroll Spinney Story* (2014), Copper Pot Pictures.

xlvi   Brian Jay Jones (2016). *Jim Henson: The Biography,* reprint edition. Ballantine Books, New York.

xlvii   C. S. Lewis (1960). *The Four Loves.* Harcourt, Brace, New York.

xlviii   http://www.businessinsider.com/8-amazing-facts-about-harriet-tubman-2016-4?pundits_only=0&get_all_comments=1&no_reply_filter=1

xlix   http://www-groups.dcs.st-and.ac.uk/history/Biographies/Rodrigues.html

l   https://www.youtube.com/watch?v=FW2Hvs5WaRY

li   http://www.slashfilm.com/cool-stuff-walt-disneys-1935-animation-manifesto/

lii   https://www.history-of-rock.com/non_frames.htm

liii   https://www.statista.com/chart/1465/vinyl-lp-sales-in-the-us/

liv   Arthur Devine (1911). "Recollection." *The Catholic Encyclopedia.* Robert Appleton Company. Retrieved March 28, 2018 from New Advent: http://www.newadvent.org/cathen/12676b.htm

About the Author

CJ Casciotta is a writer and serial media maker passionate about helping people discover and own their unique identity—or, in other words, what makes them weird. As a writer and communicator, he's traveled all over the world inspiring communities like Lululemon, the Salvation Army, TEDx, and Charity: Water. As a media director and producer, he's collaborated on projects with MGM Studios, the United Nations Foundation, and more. He created the popular podcast *Sounds Like a Movement*, which has hosted culture-shaping voices like Seth Godin, Shauna Neiquist, and Krista Tippett. In addition, CJ's work has been featured by MTV, *RELEVANT*, Catalyst, and Q Ideas. A native New Yorker, he now lives in Nashville with his wife, Kelly, and his two kids, Selah and Mack.